THE VIDAR FLAME COLUMN -

its meaning from Rudolf Steiner

Adrian Anderson Ph.D.

From the Edda to Grail Christianity

Threshold Publishing, Australia 2017
www.rudolfsteinerstudies.com

Distributed by Dennis Jones P/L - Port Campbell Press
Bayswater VIC
Australia

ISBN 978-0-9941602-9-4 paperback

Illustrations

Front cover illustration: diagram of two sides of the column

Acknowledgements

I wish to express my gratitude to the Director and staff of the *Bonn Landesmuseum*, for their help during the 1980's, accessing archive documents for my research of this statue. Apart from this help, I am in particular grateful for the kind assistance given by Museum for especially photographing the statue, in a manner that I suggested, with the aim of making more visible some features of the statue which had almost faded away.

My thanks also due to the staff of the *Bayerische Staatsbiblothek, Munich (Benützungsabteilung)*, for their assistance in locating rare documents from the 17th century which contain references relevant to the history of encounters with the Vidar (flame column) statue.

We feel ourselves to be inwardly related to the figure of Vidar, whom we are now seeking to understand in his deeper essence; and in doing this we are thereby hoping that, that which must be **the central nerve and living essence of all spiritual-science**, will be able to arise from those forces which the Archangel of the Germanic-Nordic world can contribute to the evolution of modern times...

Rudolf Steiner,
in his *Mission of Folk-Souls* lecture cycle, Oslo, 1910.

Introduction

Students of the teachings of Rudolf Steiner have an understanding that Rudolf Steiner was able to bring such unprecedented spiritual wisdom because of his closeness to Christ Jesus; and as part of this high calling, it is understood that the great archangel Michael was helping him. This Archangel is part of the Judaic-Christian religious tradition, and hence his involvement with the wisdom that Rudolf Steiner brought was culturally acceptable to his audiences, as well as feeling appropriate, so to speak.

But to the astonishment of his listeners, Rudolf Steiner revealed in a lecture given in 1910, in Norway, that there is another divine being whose inspiration brings about what he termed the "central nerve and living essence of all Spiritual Science". This spiritual being is called Vidar, and it is associated with a very different cultural context: the Scandinavian and north-European religious or spiritual cultural heritage. This heritage derives from the Druidic religion of the old Celtic peoples of Europe; their spiritual beliefs are preserved in the Edda, where Vidar has a very significant but somewhat mysterious role. He is presented as a god endowed with great spiritual power, who is pre-destined to take over the work of the highest of the gods, Odhin.

The teachings of the Druidic priesthood were cultivated in sacred places established in the great forests across the landscape of northern Europe. Their wisdom was finally written down in Iceland in medieval times, and thereby preserved for posterity, in *The Edda*. The old Druidic religion became part of the heritage of the early Christians in Europe and Britain, as the people gradually took up the new religion and the Germanic-Norse myths of the 'Old Religion' faded slowly away. Consequently as Christianity made its way into in these lands, scenes from the Edda were often carved into early churches, as either a way to show awareness of the 'Old Religion', or to show how Christianity has superceded it. The theme of such carvings predominantly focused on Odhin, Vidar and Thor at "Ragnarok", the Twilight of the Gods; see the illustration over page.

The deities and nature spirits mentioned in the Edda, are actually those experienced by the priests of the ancient Celtic-Teutonic peoples throughout central and northern Europe. For example, Rudolf Steiner reports that the deity called "Sif" was experienced and worshipped by the pre-Christian people living in central Europe. In the course of time, the clairvoyance needed for this awareness faded away from the central Europeans earlier than from the people in the northern areas. As a result, the gods of the Druidic religion of central and northern Europeans are now thought of as 'Nordic'.

So the Edda contains the old myths which preserve the esoteric-spiritual wisdom of the Druids. This tells of the activity of various divine beings, against the background of the spiritual evolving of humanity.

We know a little more about the significance of Vidar from a few striking comments he made in the course of one or two lectures from 1913 and 1914. It was in the *Folk-Souls* lecture cycle that he made the following remark,

> We feel ourselves to be inwardly related to the figure of Vidar, whom we are now seeking to understand in his deeper essence; and in doing this we are thereby hoping that, that which must be the central nerve and living essence of all spiritual-science, will be able to arise from those forces which the Archangel of the Germanic-Nordic world can contribute to the evolution of modern times...

It is made clear in the lecture that "the Archangel of the Germanic-Nordic world" is an alternative name for Vidar. Since a being who inspires or provides "the central nerve and living essence of all spiritual-science" is obviously directly working with Rudolf Steiner himself, students of anthroposophy naturally wanted to know more about this being.

In this book shall explore the nature of Vidar from all of the relevant references to him from Rudolf Steiner, and also all references to Vidar in the Edda.[1] This includes the words Vidar spoke long ago, when Lucifer had to be allowed by the gods to influence humanity; and in addition we shall consider the words he spoke to Rudolf Steiner, on two occasions. We shall also contemplate the ancient statue of Vidar which Rudolf Steiner refers to.

---

[1] There are eight references in the Poetic Edda, plus several in the Prose Edda, one of importance.

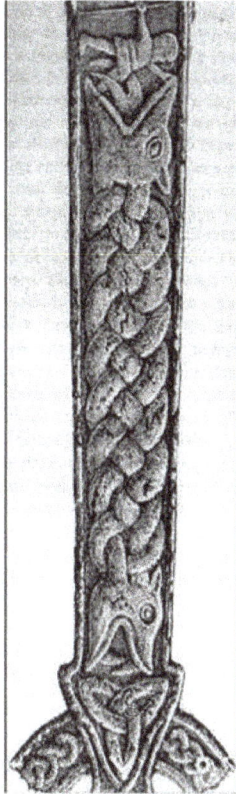

1 Nordic Gods in old Churches: Vidar or Odhin in the Ragnarok battle.
Above left/middle: the 10th century Gosforth cross, and the Vidar scene enlarged from it.
Above right: pillar in crypt of the Freisinger church, 11th century.
Below: baptism font in Freudenstadt, about 11th century.

Chapter One

The cultural-historical background

The Druidic religion

The Celtic religion included knowledge of nature spirits, Angels and Archangels, as well as influences from the stars, the sun, and the moon, especially at solstice and equinox times. This focus is apparent with the 'Nebra' disc and in the orientation of many megalithic sites in Germany and Britain. There are some brief references by Rudolf Steiner to the old clairvoyance of the Druids, which point out that they used their clairvoyance to observe cosmic energies present within the Earth's atmosphere at various times in the year. But the ancient Celts of western and northern Europe, living long before the Hellenistic Age, left little behind that explains their understanding of these things, but some knowledge of this has been learnt from the cultures that succeeded them.

The site called "The Externsteine", located in northern Germany, was the most important and powerful of all Celtic sites. Geologically, the Externsteine consists of five large, very tall rock towers amongst a distinctive outcrop in the beautiful Teutoburger Forest (in German, the Teutoburger Wald). Geologists report that this outcrop is actually several hundred metres long, although most of the rock forms don't rise up above ground level.

In 1926 this area, located in north-western Germany, encompassing 140 hectares, was made into a protected national park. The two nearest towns of any size to the Externsteine are Detmold and Paderborn.[2] It was developed primarily by the ancient Celts, but it may have been in use by indigenous people long before the Celts migrated into Western Europe (ca. 2,500 BC). It was eventually assimilated by the old Teutonic tribes people, some centuries before the Christian era.

In this second phase of its history, the time of the Roman Empire, the Externsteine played a central role in the pre-history of the later German nation. The tribal priestess and her assistants were responsible for the most decisive military defeat the Roman Empire ever suffered, at the famous battle

---

[2] For a comprehensive presentation about this site, see the book, Damien Pryor, *The Externsteine.*

of Varus in AD 9. It was in this later phase of their history, that the Druids established centres of learning throughout Gaul, and some of these sites had hundreds of acolytes in training.

In old Gaul, present-day France, some prominent education towns of today were originally Druid sites of learning which the Romans had crushed, and then re-established as Roman centres of religious and civil learning. Narbonne for example was earlier the Druid college of Narbo. There were many similar sites, such as those at Tolosa, Burdegela and Bibractis and at Alesia, now Saint Reine, just a short distance from Paris.

But the Saint Reine site was destroyed in 47 BC in the terrible and decisive battle between Gaius Julius Caesar and Vercingetorix. A few thousand acolytes either perished or fled from the clashes of their people with the brutal Romans, who were intent on conquering Western Europe. Later in 54 AD Emperor Claudius ordered the full annihilation of the Druids.

The Religion of the Druids
In the Edda, the highest of the gods is Odhin (also called Wuotan). Rudolf Steiner reveals some striking facts about this deity, which enable us to appreciate the spiritual goodness and greatness of the Druids and of the deities which are referred to in the Edda. In anthroposophy, the gods of the Edda are seen from the perspective of the nine ranks of 'hierarchies' or divine beings that sustain creation. The first three levels of beings are that of, Angels, then Archangels and then the Principalities.

The gods referred to as the "Aesir" in the Edda are Archangels and the gods referred to as the "Vanir" are Principalities. Rudolf Steiner explains that Odhin is of the rank of Principality, but he has restricted his own development to that of an Archangel, in order to be of more assistance to humanity. In fact Rudolf Steiner told his audience in Oslo, that this Archangel "took over the rulership control of the Archangelic realm" in order to work towards the fulfilment of his very important tasks on behalf of humanity.[3]

---

[3] *Folk-Souls* cycle, lecture of 14th June 1910.

In various lectures from Rudolf Steiner, the importance of Odhin is seen from the context of how the soul-life of people in earlier Ages differed from our own. In earlier ages, people were psychic, but had a less strong sense of a personal ego, but they were also tribally interlinked. That is, they felt that they all were part of the one 'group-self' or tribe.

Consequently, marriage was always amongst people of the extended tribe; (a practice called 'endogamy'). Rudolf Steiner reveals that the old psychic condition was linked to this tribal intermarriage. The great spirit-being Odhin was actively working with the problem of the need amongst human beings for a move towards the individual ego-sense.

He saw how gradually, the psychic state would diminish, if people could be moved to feel love for someone else, someone who was not part of their tribe. He therefore began to influence human souls in such a way that what was once called 'distant marriage' became acceptable. In other words, people began to feel love for persons who were not of their tribe, and hence people began to feel that they could marry outside of the tribe.[4]

Through the activity of Odhin, breaking the blood-link, a new social protocol arose and this contributed to the ending of the old psychic state of consciousness. It also meant that good-will could be felt for people beyond one's own tribe or small ethnicity, and on this basis it is not so astonishing to learn that Odhin was the inspirer of Gautama, the Buddha, the great teacher of compassion, (as well as of other especially high human beings).[5] The alternative name for Odhin in old north Germanic tongues, 'Wuotan', is the same word as 'Buddha' in old Indian languages such as Sanskrit.[6] One could say that Gautama's mission was to teach the doctrine of love or compassion. And a real love, a true good-will, is not limited to the blood-ties of one's own ethnicity; this new soul-condition was developed in human beings by Odhin.[7]

As the various folk developed, especially in Europe and around the Mediterranean shores, this 'distant-marriage'

---

[4] GA 97, lecture 29th April, 1906, p. 162.
[5] Rudolf Steiner indicated this in various lectures e.g., GA 92, p. 148, GA 105 p. 173, 199, and GA 106, p.130-132.
[6] Rudolf Steiner taught this and this linguistic conclusion is stated by Sir William Jones, (1675- 1749) a learned scholar, knowing 41 languages.
[7] But despite these cultural 'interlinkings', there is no basis to the theory that the angel of Buddha is Vidar, for Vidar is, and always has been, an Archangel.

practise lead to an enhanced individual consciousness, or sense of self, and thus eventually a more individual way of thinking. As the gods were well aware, once this capacity developed, then individual experiencing of, working with, higher ideas could arise.

We cannot go into more details about the gods of the Edda, but we can now see that Vidar belongs to a context of divine-spiritual beings, actively endeavouring to help humanity.

Chapter Two

The significance of Vidar: statements from Rudolf Steiner, and in the Edda

This is a vital question to research, because understanding of this aspect of the spiritual inspiration behind anthroposophy, enables the student of anthroposophical truths to align herself or himself more fully to the work of Rudolf Steiner. But there is another reason to earnestly contemplate the nature of this Archangel. Research into the relationship of the spiritually seeking human being and Christ Jesus, when viewed in connection with Steiner's comments about Vidar, reveals a profound mystery. We shall explore this theme in detail later, and thereby discover the reason why Vidar is spoken of with such profound veneration by Rudolf Steiner.

The name "Vidar", is of unknown meaning, which is the case with names in many languages. His realm is called "Widi"; the meaning of this word is unclear, but generally understood to have something to do with forest and wood. In terms of other symbolism, that Odhin is called the 'father' of Vidar, is to indicate that Vidar shall take over and continue the work of the lofty spiritual being Odhin, in due course.

An Icelandic tradition states that the name of his 'mother' was "Gridhr".[8] This word appears to combine the word for impetuosity (or vehemence, intensity), with the word for certainty/assurance/confidence. These are obviously opposite qualities, and so the result is: an astral reality or soul quality, of balance, where neither Ahriman nor Lucifer hold sway. Such a soul state is identified by Rudolf Steiner as a condition of high spiritual integrity, which brings the person near to the Christ-impulse.[9]

We shall start our journey of exploration into the mystery of Vidar by identifying each of the qualities of this Archangel as indicated in the Edda, and considering these in the light of the remarkable, and crucially important, *Folk-Souls* lecture cycle, given in Oslo in 1910. In my library is a copy of the original, unrevised, 1912 edition of the Folk-Souls Cycle book, as well as the official version, partly revised by Rudolf Steiner, and published in 1982 as volume 121 in his Complete Works, and

---

[8] This reference is found in the medieval *Lay of Thor*.
[9] See the lectures "*Balance in the World and Man*", (GA 158) 20-22nd Nov. 1914.

also the English version of 1970. Rudolf Steiner told his audience that those who were Scandinavians, would be interested in what he would be saying about this theme in his next lectures. The next day he began to mention the god Vidar. As we note the comments by Rudolf Steiner about Vidar, I shall refer to the different versions of these lectures where necessary.

1: Sent to Scandinavia from spiritual powers active long ago
(at the Externsteine)
In the 6th or 7th centuries AD, Vidar was sent up to Norway by the ruling spirits who were inspiring the initiated Druids at the Externsteine. This event occurred relatively shortly before this greatest of all Celtic Mystery centres, the Externsteine, was closed down, and a new centre for divine beings to guide European civilisation was established – the Castle of the Holy Grail, located above the Pyrenees Mountains of Spain.
(The *Folk-Souls* cycle; lecture, 12th June)

2: Is an Archangel, and known as such in Atlantean times
Vidar is an Archangel who is actually at the stage where he is virtually at the rank of a Principality. In the 7th lecture of the *Folk-Souls* cycle, Rudolf Steiner begins to refer to Vidar, without using his name. He refers to him as the "Nordic Folk-Archangel",

> ..this Nordic Folk-Archangel who indeed has the inner configuration in itself, in a certain sense, to ascend up to the rank of an Archai {already}... (Lecture, 12th June)[10]

The migrating of Folk-spirits, mentioned above, was known to Rudolf Steiner years before the invaluable *Folk-Souls* cycle was given. In 1905, brief notes of a lecture report this,

> ...with the Roman State the {concept of} legal Rights was developed; there, this became permeated by Christian [theological] ideas. Christianity had the duty, in that cultural Epoch to develop the Greeks in regard to the external world {of Nature}, the Romans for the realm of ethics, and the later civilisations {in Europe} in regard to an inner religiosity. And later the Nordic

---

[10] The theory of Vidar being only an Angel until the time of Buddha is incompatible with these words of Rudolf Steiner.

peoples each received their mission {from a Christ-inspired influence}.[11]

It is taught in the 1910 *Folk-Souls* cycle that these Nordic peoples were each guided by a Folk-Spirit, and in this way "received their mission". It is above all in the *Folk-Souls* cycle where Rudolf Steiner explains that what we can call a 'Folk-Spirit' is a deity of the rank of Archangel.[12] This situation, and the role of these Archangels in the way that history has unfolded between different nations, is explained in detail in the *Folk-Souls* cycle.

That Archangels are beings who have existed as such since remote Ages is quite clearly pointed out in many of Rudolf Steiner's works. That Vidar is one such Archangel is stated in the crucial words from Rudolf Steiner which are placed at the beginning of the book,

> ...that from out of the host of ancient spirit-beings, Vidar shall again appear, in a new form.

This same truth was affirmed in other lectures,

> The primal Germanic-Nordic people of Europe saw these spirit hosts in the early post-Atlantean times, and {consequently} the European Mysteries were then established.[13]

This tells us that the actual beginnings of the Celtic-Druidic wisdom goes back to about 7000 BC. But elsewhere Rudolf Steiner tells us that the Nordic gods, hence Vidar, were also known in Atlantean times,

> The ancestors of these old Nordic-Germanic peoples saw Odhin and the other gods {including Vidar} in the Atlantean epoch.[14]

3: A 'pagan' deity who became 'Christian' about AD 600
But we note here, that it is clear from the above extract from the *Folk-Souls* cycle, that the esoteric Christian Grail centre and its guiding Spirits were behind this dispensing of a

---

[11] Lecture, 24th Oct., 1905.
[12] S. Prokofieff decided that Vidar was an Angel until ca. 500BC: see Appendices Seven and Eight for more about this.
[13] GA 103, p. 42.

[14] GA 106, p. 130.

mission to various Scandinavian Folk-Spirits. It is also clear from this, that Vidar was sent up to Norway about the 6th - 7th centuries AD, just as we noted earlier.

But it was not until 1923 that Rudolf Steiner revealed a core truth about this great Archangel, namely that it was around the same time, approximately AD 600, when Vidar was given his mission in Norway, that he **became "converted" to Christianity, and thus ceased to be a 'pagan' deity so to speak,**

> After the mystery of Golgotha, humanity must strive to make this experience of an en-souled, spiritualized nature {thus the seasonal cycle with its various nature spirits} constitute the following of Christ...for the nature spirits can all be seen in the following of Christ, but without Him they cannot be seen. This however, is indicated precisely here {in Norway} in that the people here were informed about this – that from out of the host of ancient spirit- beings, Vidar shall again appear, in a new form:
> **Vidar, after he has converted himself to Christianity,** shall again appear out of the host of ancient divine beings.[15]
>
> (Emphasis mine, A.A.)

This matter of Vidar becoming a 'Christian' being, that is, a spiritual being who has attuned itself to the Christ-impulse, only after some centuries into the Christian era, was in fact already suggested in the *Folk-Souls* cycle itself, when Rudolf Steiner speaks of the significance of,

> ...how this Archangel's potentiality to influence humanity will develop, after he has had the benefit of being 'educated' by the Christian Time-Spirit. (lecture, 17th June)

A 'Time-Spirit' is a Principality; these beings rule over an entire cultural, zodiacal epoch (which lasts for 2,160 years). Here we can see that Vidar is an Archangel, deeply associated with Nordic-Druidic wisdom, and with the spirit beings who sustain the natural world.[16]

---

[15] GA 226, lecture in Oslo, 21st May, 1923.
[16] The theory that Vidar was the Christian-Biblical 'Angel of the Lord', is fully incompatible with these words of Rudolf Steiner.

4: Vidar is the Folk-Spirit of Norway

We have established that Vidar is an Archangel, and known as such since time immemorial, and that he was sent up to Scandinavia about AD 600 as one of several Folk-Spirits. People have often wondered just what country is Vidar then associated with? To answer this, we have to firstly note that Rudolf Steiner was reluctant to use the name, Vidar.

Secondly, he did not want to create any rivalry amongst the Scandinavians in his audience, so in the course of the lectures, he used several titles for Vidar. It was only in 1914, when he was back in Germany, that he revealed that Vidar is also the Folk-Spirit of Norway. In this lecture, he speaks of how, in his quest for deeper understanding of the Holy Grail, he put a question to a certain Folk-Spirit,

> when some time ago, I questioned the Norwegian Folk-Spirit, the Nordic Folk-Spirit, about Parsifal...[17]

Now, in the *Folk-Souls* cycle he called Vidar "the Nordic Folk-Archangel", (p. 132 in the 1982 German edition), and also "the Archangel of the Germanic-North", and also "Folk-Spirit in the North" (these all on p. 189) and later, "the Nordic-Germanic Archangel" (p. 196). However, on page 196, in one long sentence, he uses this term, "the Nordic-Germanic Archangel" interchangeably **as another name for Vidar**. Then on page 197, he again refers to "the Nordic-Germanic Archangel"; and by now it is clear that this is one of several terms for Vidar.

So we can now confirm that the term, "the Nordic Folk-Spirit" in the above sentence from 1914, "*...I questioned the Norwegian Folk-Spirit, the Nordic Folk-Spirit, about Parsifal...*" means exactly the same as "Folk-Spirit in the North" or "the Nordic-Germanic Archangel" – all confirmed in Rudolf Steiner's Oslo lectures as alternative terms for Vidar.

Later on, when Rudolf Steiner was once again back in Oslo, in 1921, and again at the 'Vidar' branch, he referred to the *Folk-Souls* cycle, and shows his reluctance to speak the name Vidar,

> This is actually the reason that the anthroposophical group here bears its name, a name that we have, some years ago earlier, spoken here.

---

[17] GA 149, *Christ and the spiritual World*, lecture, 1st Jan. 1914.

A few minutes later, he uses the term "Nordic Spirit" in a way that appears to be a similar expression to those above. He told his audience,

> ...that if right here in Norway, **that** will be developed, for which the Nordic Spirit is very especially talented, then here can ripen an understanding which can work to fructify anew the rest of the western world.[18]

Here we see, from these brief statements, that Vidar is an Archangel, whose name one should not speak too freely, and who is also the Folk-Spirit of the Norwegian people.

5: Vidar is closely associated with the spiritual ideas and pictures embedded in the Edda, including Druidic awareness of the spiritual reality behind creation

The Edda derives from the spiritual initiation knowledge and clairvoyance of the ancient Druids. It tells of the creation of the world, and the role of various deities, including malignant ones, in the world. It also tells of the intrusion into the human world of the malignant Loki, (who is Lucifer), and how he brings darkness over the world of the gods. The Edda also looks to the future, and includes an apocalyptic element which foretells a time when humanity can no longer perceive and respond to the gods.

Then a mighty spiritual war begins, in the time of the 'Fimbul' winter; it tells us of how the greatest of the Gods, Odhin, dies in this war, but then Vidar, who has been waiting silently in the background, steps forward. He then avenges Odhin, by destroying the evil powers (The Fenris Wolf) and eventually a new Golden Age begins. We have noted above that the greatest sacred site of the Druidic initiates was The Externsteine, which is located in a remote forest area of northern Germany, not far from Detmold and Paderborn. As the book, *The Externsteine*[19] shows, this ancient site is subtly referred to in the Edda itself,

> Easy it is for those who come to Odhin
> to recognize his hall –
> an outcast* is placed   (*lit. a wolf)
> to the west of the door,

---

[18] GA 209, lecture, 24th Nov. 1921. The term 'Nordic Spirit' can mean either the Nordic mind-set of people, or in effect, 'the Archangel of the North'.
[19] *The Externsteine,* by Damien Pryor.

and an eagle hovers above.

(Author's trans. Grimnismal 10)

Above the large grotto inside the main rock wall of this site, an eagle has been carved, long ago. And to the west of this is the figure of Nidhoggr: the symbol of the lower sensuality of the human soul. Something very intriguing occurs here in this verse from the Edda. As I mentioned in the *Rudolf Steiner Handbook*, the Druidic priests who composed these verses used a word here for 'wolf' which is different to the ordinary, everyday term in old Icelandic for wolf (*ulfr*), such as when the verses speak about the wolf Skioll.

It is the word, *vargr*, which derives from the term for warning, or an admonition, *vara*. Here it has the meaning of an outcast, that is, an entity not welcome in the community. The menacing sight of Nidhoggr ensnaring two people is referring to this 'outcast': that is, to people who have not yet overcome their lower qualities.[20]

It is clear from Rudolf Steiner's remarks, that the Externsteine has been closed down, spiritually, long ago; that is, it is no longer a functioning sacred site because the divine beings who once were involved with the Druids, withdrew as the esoteric Christian impulse arose. The spiritual guidance of Europe was then directed from the mysterious Holy Grail centre. But from the Druids, and all that they experienced, the later Teutonic peoples inherited the very rich 'faery lore'.

Vidar has a close connection with the 'world of faery' and the involvement of nature spirits in the seasonal cycle, such as we find in the stories of the Edda, and in Scandinavian folk-tales. We also find glimpses of this in old British faery-lore, presented in Shakespeare's *Midsummer Night's Dream*.[21] As the quote we gave earlier in this chapter demonstrates,

> After the mystery of Golgotha, humanity must strive to make this experience of an en-souled, spiritualized nature {thus the seasonal cycle with its various nature spirits} constitute the following of Christ...for the nature spirits can all be seen in the following of Christ, but without Him they cannot be seen. This however, is indicated precisely here {in Norway} in that the people

---

[20] To read more about the Externsteine, see *The Externsteine* Damien Pryor.
[21] This is the literary work which is responsible for keeping alive knowledge of the world of faery in the English-speaking world.

here were informed about this – that from out of the host of ancient spirit-beings, Vidar shall again appear, in a new form...

It is here that we can discern that a high spiritual being, who is closely involved with the hosts of nature sprites and other beings who maintain the natural, seasonal life-cycles of our planet, is also a being very close to the cosmic Christ. So, the 'pagan' world and 'Christ-associated' realities have merged in the being of the Archangel. And it is precisely this which underlies the radical new teachings of Rudolf Steiner about the new cycle of festivals which spiritually insightful individuals could work together to create. Underlying these new festivals, which interweave the cosmic Christ's influence in the seasonal cycles sustained by the realm of 'faery', is inspiration from this great Archangel.

6: This Archangel has held back its own potential

As we noted earlier, Vidar is an Archangel who is actually at the stage where he is virtually the rank of a Principality,

> ..this Archangel who indeed has the inner configuration in itself, in a certain sense, to ascend up to the rank of an Archai {already}... (Lecture, 12th June)

So, in a past age, the Archangel Vidar kept back; that is, consciously held back, certain capacities which he has, in order that at some later time these capacities could strengthen his ability to help humanity. This holding back of his power, and also awaiting for him to be given a fuller power than is normally his, is emphasized in the edited version of the lectures in the *Folk-Souls* cycle. In the transcript of his lectures, as published in 1911, Rudolf Steiner told his audience,

> the Nordic mythology presents the original aptitude and abilities of this Archangel, who was sent up here to the north: the original aptitude and abilities, {thus} being what we would seek for in a human child in the way of talents or genius.[22]

In editing this passage, that is improving the text for a later publication, Rudolf Steiner added further words to emphasize this holding back of a capacity (added words in bold fonts),

---

[22] *Die Mission einzelner Volksseelen...* Lect, 12th June (pm), p.10, Berlin, 1911Philosophischer-anthroposophischer Vlg.

the Nordic mythology presents the original aptitude and abilities of this Archangel, who was sent up here to the north: the original aptitude and abilities, **which in their configuration have remained static**, {thus} being what we would have to seek for in a child, if certain talents, latent genius and so forth, **remain at the childhood state.**[23]

As we shall see, the time for the stepping forward of Vidar, to influence humanity, has now arrived.

A passage from the Edda, points to this refraining from exerting his full power; it is in "Loki's Quarrel", where we learn that, as the gods gather in their great hall, the evil god 'Loki' appears, and demands to be part of the gathering. In other words, the time has come when Lucifer's influence has to enter into humanity's evolving. To facilitate this, the great leader of the Gods, Odhin, has to request that Vidar arises and leaves the banquet table, to make a seat available for Loki,

> So get up, Vidar, to make a place
> for the father of the Wolf,
> That never shall Loki speak maliciously
> against us here in the hall of the Aesir.

> (Loki's Quarrel v.10)

Unless Vidar retreats – that is, holds back from exerting his full capacity – the fallen spirits which bring about evil, cannot gain access to humanity's soul-life. Vidar here is obviously given a very high spiritual status; this situation is affirmed by Rudolf Steiner's words that Vidar has the capacity to rise already to the rank of Principality, but has remained back, to help humanity. This aspect of Vidar will be explored later in the book. Knowledge of this aspect of Vidar resulted in him being called "the silent god" by the Druids, as shown in a later section of the Edda (*Gylfaginning* 29).

Later, we shall see that there is another reason for this high status being accorded to him in ancient times. This has to do with his future tasks wherein he becomes closely associated with the Christ-Impulse. This verse from the Edda also shows that the Druids had knowledge of a core spiritual truth which

---

[23] *Die Mission einzelner Volksseelen...* Lect, 12th June, Berlin 1922 & Dornach 1962, p.133.

is known in anthroposophy; namely that Ahriman (the Fenris Wolf of Nordic Mythology) is the karmic result of Lucifer (Loki) affecting humanity. In other words, once Lucifer gains access to humanity (or to individual persons), this opens the door to Ahriman to have influence also.

7: Vidar is closely connected to the Scandinavian myths

Rudolf Steiner reveals that the various Scandinavian Archangels are directly influenced by the degree of understanding that human beings can develop for the Edda, for the old Nordic-Germanic myths. He taught that these Archangels (which includes Vidar),

> ...embody those potentialities which were later expressed in the especial configuration of Scandinavian mythology. Herein lies the special importance of Scandinavian mythology for the understanding of the real, inner being of the Scandinavian Folk-Souls.   (Lecture, 12th June.)

This particular feature clarifies a similar statement made by Rudolf Steiner some years earlier, and preserved in an archive document:

> There is nothing within the knowledge that derives from the Mysteries which can also lead a person so deeply into the theosophical way of thinking, as the Nordic legends and sagas. If the European can live into this, he or she can from that entry point, penetrate ever further into the esoteric area of life.[24]

The material which he is referring to here is primarily the texts preserved in the Edda. We note too, that Rudolf Steiner specifies the European peoples, and we can conclude that he is including Anglo-Saxon peoples; in other words, if one's ethnicity has its origins in the European-Celtic peoples, then one's astral body would resonate to these stories.

There is a passage in the Edda which alludes to the link between the Archangel Vidar and the poetic, mantric verses and sayings that eventually came to be known as the Edda. It occurs immediately after Vidar is requested to arise and step back from the table, to allow Loki access. As he does this, he

---

[24] Lecture, 22nd March 1905.

speaks the following words, and specifically points to a god called Bragi, who had just voiced his opposition to Loki,

> Blessed fortune and well-being for the Aesir gods,
> and for the Aesir goddesses,
> and to all of the most sacred gods – except for one,
> who is seated further in, on the bench of Bragi.

(Loki's Quarrel v. 11)

The god Bragi is the god responsible for inspiring those who, like the central European Minnesingers, told stories derived from the ancient Mystery wisdom, in poetic verses and obscure sayings. So here Vidar is pointing to a regrettable weakening of the power of Bragi. He is thereby alluding to the future decline of this Mystery wisdom, as Luciferic forces take hold of the human soul ever more. (To see why I view this verse as spoken by Vidar, rather than by Loki (the traditional view), see Appendix Eight.

8: This Archangel is the inspirer of those who seek to achieve deep spirituality today

Rudolf Steiner begins to unveil the secrets of Vidar in the *Folk-Souls* cycle at the end of the lecture of 15th June, when he indicates that Druidic initiates said to their students, that it was important that he or she "should become a son {or daughter} of Odhin". He explains that this phrase refers to becoming inwardly aligned to Vidar, who was called "the son of Odhin", because he was pre-destined to take over the role of Odhin in guiding humanity, at that apocalyptic time when Ahriman enters strongly into world history.

That time, referred to as the "Ragnarok" era in the Edda, is now; that is, the modern era is the 'Twilight of the Gods'. This phrase refers to the time when an earth-bound, non-holistic, non-clairvoyant consciousness would take over many people. The kind of higher consciousness that earlier existed, is glimpsed in an esoteric passage from the old Nordic texts, called *Odhin's Runes-song*. It describes an initiation experience that a leading initiate in the Druidic world underwent: someone who was a human vessel of their highest god, Odhin,

> ....I know that I hung on a windy Tree nine nights long;
> wounded by the spear, consecrated to Odhin,
> I myself consecrated to myself:
> on that tree of which

20

no one knows from what root it grows.
They gave me neither food nor drink,
I lowered myself down, took up the runes,
groaning I took them up, then fell I to the earth....
spiritually I grew and I thrived;
wise became I.
From a word unto word was I led to word;
from deed unto deed was I led to deed.

(Author's trans.)

Rudolf Steiner taught that this initiation was undergone in the ancient Indian Epoch (7227-5067 BC). The person who underwent this ordeal was described by Rudolf Steiner as someone who was a great initiate already in the Atlantean Age.[25] He had also been responsible for bringing over to North-western Europe the core spiritual wisdom of the Atlantean people.[26] The tree on which Odhin was 'hanging' was no doubt, the famous Tree of All-life symbolizing creation, mentioned often in the Edda, and called *Yggdrasil*. The famous 'Irmin' column of the Celts, which was taken over by the Teutonic people, and which once existed at the Externsteine, was a symbol of this. This column was a tall wooden carving which depicted the nine layers of creation.

To be 'hanging on the tree' is therefore a metaphor for an initiated priest merging his consciousness with cosmic realities; the 'tree' being the Tree of Life, the cosmos itself. This was a process that no doubt was carried out with difficulty, requiring considerable tenacity. Rudolf Steiner taught that later, another high initiate of the Druidic world, known as Sieg, was also re-named "Odhin" because he had achieved the high spirituality that is associated with the leader of their Gods.[27] It is a process of this type, in a new form, which the Archangel Vidar now makes possible for the spiritual seeker.

A passage from the Edda affirms that this Archangel is very significant to those on the path to spiritual development of an esoteric kind,

If you have a friend
who you deeply trust,
go often, to seek him out,
for tussocks grow, and long grass,

---

[25] Archive lecture, 22nd March 1905.
[26] Archive lecture, 21st Oct. 1904.
[27] Ditto

in Vidar's forest region.

(The Sayings of Loddfafnir)

The implication here is that Vidar is not normally accessible, and only the few, those few that seek higher consciousness, make the effort to find this deity. There is a further text in the Edda, which refers to the 'becoming a son of Odhin", that is, a person who is close to Vidar. The text is from the *Voluspa* or the *Seeress' Prophecy*, about the Ragnarok time, when Vidar is to become active. The line in verse 55 is preserved only in a fragmentary way, but this much is clear,

> Vidar's kin mean death to the Wolf.

In other words, those who take up the path to spirituality, in the time of ahrimanic materialism and decadence, are helping to weaken the power of Ahriman.

9: To the ancient Druids, Vidar had a future mission of extraordinary importance.
A feature of this Archangel is that he is considered so sacred, that the Druids were reluctant to use his name. And, as we have seen, Rudolf Steiner also was noticeably reluctant use his name, except where necessary for clarity.

In the Edda is a powerful text that I mentioned in the *Rudolf Steiner Handbook*, which is directly about Vidar, showing him as more powerful than Odhin, with a future mission, but avoids using his name,

> A noble one* came forth to us,   (* Odhin) [28]
> greater than all others,
> the Earth empowered this son,
> He was declared the most endowed of rulers,
> Through kin, kinship had he with all the Powers. [29]

> One day another shall come forth,

---

[28] The old Icelandic text: Varð einn borinn, öllum meiri, sá var aukinn jarðar megni; þann kveða stilli stórúðgastan sif sifjaðan sjötum görvöllum.
Þá kemr annarr enn máttkari, þó þori ek eigi þann at nefna; fáir séa nú fram of lengra en Óðinn mun ulfi mæta.
Usually the text reads, "a man was born" but the old Icelandic verb here 'bera' often has entirely other meanings, such as 'to bring towards', 'raised on high towards', 'carried forth'.
[29] Usually "...kinship had he with all the tribes/families". But since Odhin was a deity, spiritual powers are intended here; and the word 'sjölum', old Danish for spiritual powers (or earthly dynasties) occurs as a reliable variant reading to sjötum (tribes) in the pivotal Codex Regius.

Mightier than he,
But to name him I dare not,
Few now gaze further ahead than
when Odhin encounters the wolf.   (Hyndla's Song)

Another reference in the Edda emphasizes this waiting of
Vidar, until the apocalyptic times arrive when humanity will
need help to achieve a spiritual renewal,

Tussocks grow and long grass
in Vidar's forest region,
there the son,
on the back of the steed,
courageously makes it known[30]
he shall avenge the father.
                    (Grimnir's Sayings v.15)

10: Anthroposophy shall inaugurate the mission of Vidar who seeks to nurture a new clairvoyance in people

It is in the last lecture (17th June 1910) of the *Folk-Souls* cycle
that we find most of the indications about this Archangel. The
first indication is somewhat carefully worded,

that which constitutes such imagery {of the Edda}
derives from the initiates {Druids} and has been
interwoven, or inserted into, the Folk-soul, into the
general feelings and attitudes of the people {of the
North}. Consequently very much indeed remains in the
leading Archangel, in the Folk-Spirit of the North {i.e.,
Vidar} of that which was the old {spiritual-esoteric}
educational process, {achieved} clairvoyance. Much
remains of that which could develop in a person who,
in their evolving within the physical world, connects
themselves to a clairvoyant development process.

But later in this lecture he makes a very clear, direct
statement that the new clairvoyance derives from this great
Archangel,

Those who are called upon to elucidate, from the signs
of the times, that which must come to pass, they know
the new spiritual research {Anthroposophy} will re-
establish the power of Vidar, who shall banish from

---

[30] The Old Icelandic verb, 'geverte', ('makes it known') has many nuances, and
here it implies that a priestess/priest, in perceiving Vidar, receives awareness
of his intentions.

the hearts and minds of people all the dark, confusing relics of the old clairvoyance. and shall awaken in the human soul the new clairvoyance that is gradually unfolding.

The importance of Vidar for those who seek to develop their higher consciousness can scarcely be exaggerated. Similarly, the closeness of Vidar to Rudolf Steiner, and to the arising of anthroposophical wisdom in people, is hard to exaggerate.

11: Vidar inspires community-based quests for spirituality
We noted earlier the words which Vidar spoke, as given in the Edda, in the early stages in humanity's evolution, when Loki demanded access to the human soul. In the last lecture of the *Folk-Souls* cycle, Rudolf Steiner reports a brief comment actually made by Vidar to him, in the spiritual worlds. He revealed this to the audience,

> And if higher spiritual forces are to be awakened in mankind in the future, which we certainly shall see come about before our eyes, then, {to use the words of Vidar, the Aesir who has been silent until now}, *he will become the active friend of cooperative work or cooperative endeavour,* in the same sense that we have all gathered here.

We shall consider the other words spoken by Vidar to Rudolf Steiner, when we explore the relation of this Archangel to the Holy Grail.

12: He helps in this Ahrimanic time of darkness
A prominent feature of Vidar in the Edda is that he steps in, to help humanity in the "Ragnarok" time – the Twilight of the Gods. This means that he fights against the Fenris Wolf, which represents the ahrimanic powers. The Edda has a focus on that future Age when the gods are no longer part of humanity's consciousness. The *Voluspa* or the *Seeress's Prophecy*, has a quality reminiscent of the Book of Revelation, and culminates in a description of an apocalyptic battle between the evil powers and the gods. At this point in the narrative, the all-important role of Vidar is emphasized. He is described as becoming greater than the ruler of the gods, Odhin, who is killed in the battle,

> Then the great son of the Victory-Father comes –

Vidar – to fight against the son of the giant,
with his hand he stabs his sword
through the gaping jaws, to the heart,
thus does he avenge Odhin.

Rudolf Steiner refers to this perception, seen long ago by Druidic seers, in the following way,

> The power given by the old Archangel Odhin, the old clairvoyant powers, cannot save man {in the time of Ragnarok}; something very different must supplant them. These future powers are known to Teutonic mythology: it is fully aware of their existence. It knows that the etheric form exists in which shall be embodied that which we are destined to see again – Christ, in an etheric form. He alone shall succeed in banishing the dark and impure clairvoyant powers which would confuse mankind if Odhin were not to succeed in overcoming the Fenris Wolf {which symbolizes the atavistic clairvoyance}. Vidar, who has been silent until now, shall overcome the Fenris Wolf.
>
> Whoever recognizes the significance of Vidar and feels this being in his soul, will find that in {as of} the twentieth century, the power to see the Christ can be given to mankind again. Vidar, who is part of the heritage of Northern and Central Europe shall again be visible to people.[31]

These are extraordinary words which have fascinated students of anthroposophy ever since they were spoken. These words appear to identify Vidar with Christ. The Fenris Wolf is defined in the *Folk-Souls* cycle in various ways; here the implication is that the old, somewhat unreliable clairvoyance, which can be used by negative spirit beings, and is therefore defined as the Fenris Wolf. This is no doubt, to emphasize the superiority and importance of the new clairvoyance.

His next words refer to a carving that was made of this god; see the next section. Before we consider the carving of Vidar, we need to note that there is another reference to Vidar which concerns his shoe, and how he places his foot in the jaws of the Fenris Wolf, to destroy it.

---

[31] We see again, from these words that Vidar is not an Angel associated with India, and the Bible, but an ancient Archangel associated with the Celtic world since long ages.

13: Vidar uses a thick shoe to conquer the Fenris Wolf

Gylfaginning (51) has this description of the apocalyptic battle; that is, the era when the ahrimanic powers become strong. This refers to the modern era in which a materialistic, lack of interest in the spiritual worlds predominates,

> The Fenris Wolf swallows Odhin at Ragnarok, bringing his death immediately. Vidar then approaches the Wolf and places his shoe upon the wolf's lower jaw. On this foot he has that shoe which is constantly being formed from the scraps of leather which people cast away from their shoes, as they are being made; especially from the toes and heels. Therefore everyone should cast away those scraps, who is concerned with helping the gods. With his hands, Vidar then grasps the Wolf by the upper jaw and tears his snout apart. And that is the death of the Fenris Wolf.

This reference takes us into deeply esoteric themes, which is explored in Appendix One. In illustration 3, I attempt to make clear the features which originally existed on the statue of Vidar. In the next chapter we shall start with regard to this statue, with establishing just which statue was Rudolf Steiner referring to, and the very first historical notice of its existence, as well as the first ever drawings made of it. We shall see how gradually it came to the attention of modern experts in Celtic artwork, which existed long before the early Teutonic tribes.

Chapter Three

The Druids' esoteric carving of Vidar

Towards the end of the last chapter of the *Folk-Souls* cycle, Rudolf Steiner makes a fascinating statement about an ancient Druidic carving designed to depict Vidar esoterically,

> (Vidar, who is part of the heritage of Northern and Central Europe shall again be visible to people.) He was kept secret in the Mysteries and secret schools, as a god who would receive his mission only in the future. Only vague comments were uttered even about the image made of him. It may well be due to this fact, that a depiction of him was found in the vicinity of Cologne, of which no-one knows whom it portrays, but which is nothing other than an image of Vidar.

These intriguing words from Rudolf Steiner led some enterprising anthroposophists, early in the twentieth century, to search for this artwork with initiative and alertness; and they were successful.[32] There were four main facts from Rudolf Steiner that they had to bear in mind in their search.

One:
We are told that, "he was kept secret" and "only vague comments" were made about him, including about any depiction made of him. This means that his actual nature remained unknown. It also means that any artistic depiction of him would involve features which would not be associated with what was understood in the broader community about Vidar. It was not a secret that Vidar had an association with slaying evil beings.

In other words, since only vague comments were made about his future mission and appearance, any esoteric depiction of him would not be recognized. So an artistic depiction of this Archangel had to be different to what would be easily recognizable. What is easily recognizable about Vidar are, depictions showing him on a horse with a spear, waiting for the time of Ragnarok; or fighting the Fenris Wolf with his feet in its jaws, or having a special shoe. The Druids could not keep secret, and unrecognizable, any such artwork that showed him in either of these states, because the Celtic

---

[32] For example, Hans Gesänger and Rudolf Meyer, researching in the 1930's onwards, mentioned the correct carving in the books written in the 1960's.

people would easily recognize that. Such recognizable depictions of Vidar do exist (see illustration 1). So, the statue that had been found would not be recognizably a depiction of Vidar – except to the initiate Rudolf Steiner, or to someone who had studied anthroposophy.

Two:
The carving has to have been found "near Cologne" – but we need to bear in mind that Rudolf Steiner was saying these things to an international audience of Theosophists gathered in Oslo. Smaller towns like Bonn or Koblenz, or a village like Pfalzfeld or St, Goar, etc, would have been unknown to most of his listeners. Pfalzfeld and St. Goar are "near to" Cologne, when viewed from the distant location of Oslo.

Three:
The artwork had to be renowned, and quite formally described as mysterious, and hence enigmatic, by experts in the field. It had to be a clear fact that, despite numerous efforts, archaeologists or art historians could not succeed in assessing it, and thus identifying whom it depicted. So, this statue must have been widely proclaimed and yet remained enigmatic to archaeologists and art historians.

Four:
It is a Nordic-Germanic-Celtic deity, especially depicted by Druidic initiates; it would not be a Roman, Greek or Teutonic work of art.

As we shall see in the next chapter, the earlier anthroposophical researchers were successful; they found a statue in a museum in the small town of Bonn which meets all these conditions. It is in fact the only artwork which meets all of these conditions.[33] See illustration 2, for examples of readily identifiable depictions of heroic Nordic deities.

We shall now explore the correct image of Vidar, to become familiar with the history of its discovery and re-discovery over the centuries, and what its symbolic features tell us about the deity who through Rudolf Steiner brought anthroposophy into the world.

---

[33] S. Prokofieff decided that a crude post-Celtic gravestone, for a Teutonic chieftain, was the right stone: an artefact identified as such by archaeologists.

2 Depictions of Nordic gods that are recognizable as such.
Above: Tangelgarda stone; 7th century in Gotland: Odhin leading
his warriors. Below left: Altuna Viking stone; Thor in a boat
fighting the Midgard serpent. Below right: Thorwald's Cross;
Isle of Man, probably depicting Odhin fighting the Fenris Wolf.

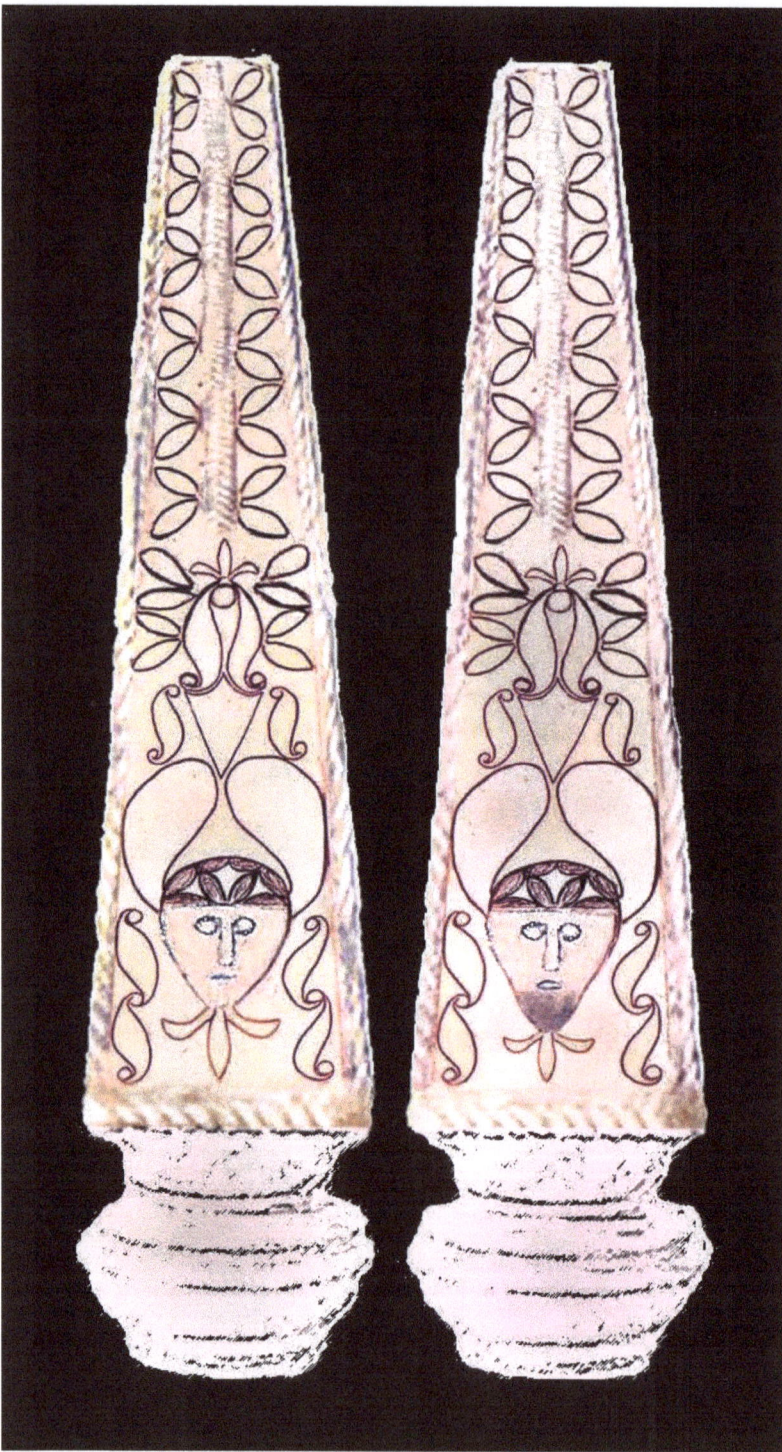

3 Two of the four sides of the reconstructed column
Two sides each depict the mouth closed and no beard; the other two sides each have the mouth open and a beard.

My sketch of the Vidar carving, in illustration 3, is based on extensive research into this statue, and how it appeared in an illustration made some 400 years ago, and also in the 1700's, and in a drawing and a professional photograph taken in 1901. The sketch is also based on the outcome of photography made by technicians in the museum, according to my suggestions, to the Director of the Bonn Landesmuseum, where the original statue is located. We shall examine the features of the sketch, after having become familiar with the history and appearance of the carving over the past 400 years.

The first report and first drawing of the statue: 1608
In the year 1607-08, an accomplished scholar, Wilhelm Dilich, who was a skilled illustrator, was commissioned by the Landgrave of the county, Moritz the Learned, son of Philip II, to make drawings of "Scenes of the County", being all his castles and other buildings. So, Dilich travelled throughout the beautiful countryside of the county of Hesse, to record in etchings its features. Walking through the magnificent scenery of the Rhineland, with its vineyards covering the hills and valleys, not very far south of Cologne, he came across the tiny village of Pfalzfeld, a few kilometres from the Rhine River and not far from a fortified castle, *Rheinfels.*

There in this quiet village, he stopped to ponder a remarkable sandstone carving in the church grounds. It stood several metres high, and was such an intriguing object that he drew a picture of it to include in his magnificent folio of drawings or maps, *Geographical maps of the localities of Hesse between the Rhine and Weser rivers 1607-1622.*[34] It is very noticeable from the drawing by Dilich, that long ago, this statue was about two metres taller, see illustrations 4 and 5.

For the first time in the modern (i.e., post-Renaissance) world, someone had brought knowledge of this remarkable carving to the world's attention; see illustration 6 for a map showing Pfalzfeld in the Rhineland. It had been erected in a Celtic sacred site, some 2,000 years earlier, but in 1608, archaeologists and historians had no knowledge of the old Celtic cultures, which had long since disappeared. So the significance of Dilich's discovery went unnoticed by most people, as the illustration he drew was not recognized.

---

[34] *Landtafeln hessischer Ämter zwischen Rhein und Weser 1607-1622.*

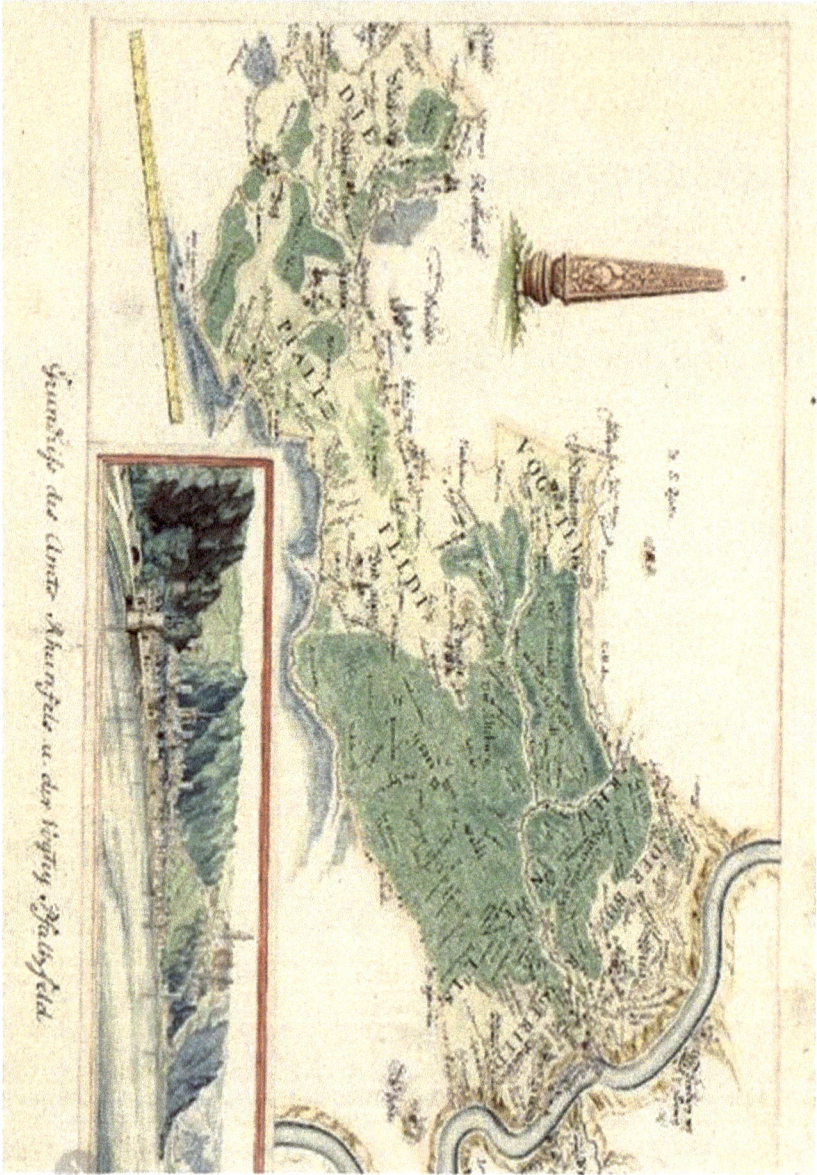

4 Map of the area from 1608, where the statue was found by
   W. Dilich

5 Drawing of the Vidar statue, from 1608, by W. Dilich.

6 Pfalzfeld village in the Rhineland: marked by a red circle. Once a sacred Celtic mystery site, the Vidar statue was set up here, about 500 BC. Later a church was built on the site, perhaps already in the 9th century.

For example, in the 1670's, an Englishman, a certain Dr. E. Browne, went on a journey through Germany, and published a book, *Travels in Europe*; and he spoke of his brief stay in the village of St. Goar which he called, "A pleasant town belonging to the Landgrave of Hesse". But he was not told anything about the strange carving which was not far away, in Pfalzfeld.[35]

The Second report of the Statue
Some forty years after Dilich, in 1649, a famous German scholar, Johann Just Winckelmann, also traveled through Germany, to record the significant features and history of the counties. He specifically mentions this strange column, but made no drawing of it. In his book, published many years later, in 1697, he writes,

> In the county of Hesse, lies a very weathered and un-inhabited village, called 'Pfalzfeld', in which I found in the year 1649, on 15th July, in the church grounds, surrounded by tussocks and thorns and thistles, a very old Roman monument. It was in the form of a 'flame-column', only about 3.5 yards long, with various **non-recognizable features** and without any inscription.[36]   (Emphasis mine, A.A.)

The village had been emptied of most of its inhabitants because of the Thirty Years' War. But Winckelmann's experience did have an impact in the county of Hesse-Rheinfels-Rotenburg, even before his book was published, for the next event in the investigation of this artwork occurred in 1690.

Third Report about the statue: 1690
This was an investigation amongst the villagers, called for by Landgrave Ernest, (1623-1693) the ruler of this county, as to what they recalled of the column.[37] Landgrave Ernst was very interested in the assets and features of his county, especially the great castle Rheinfels. He spent the vast sum of 2 million Talers in refurbishing it, (by comparison a skilled artisan was

---

[35] Dr. E. Browne, Travels in Europe, B. Tooke, London, 1687.

[36] Page 119 of, Johann Just Winkelmanns Gründliche Wahrhafte Beschreibung der Fürstenthümer Hessen und Hersfeld.... Gedruckt von H. Brauer, im Jahr 1697, Bremen.

[37] Alexander Grebel, Geschichte der Stadt St. Goar, Druck von Carl Cassenroth, 1848.

35

paid about 7 Talers per week at that time).[38] A brief notice of his investigation was published in a book about the history of St. Goar, by Alexander Grebel. Grebel, born in Koblenz 1907 - died in St. Goar in 1870, was a distinguished historian of the local area. He worked as a lawyer and was a member of the local Parliament, and wrote three books on the local area's history.

He reports that the outcome of the investigation of 1690 was, that the villagers thought that this column derived from 'the old pagan times', especially as the old people of the village reported that they believe that "still in the year 1648, at the top of the column there was a head, shaped like that of a human being, but that this part had since come off from the column". Actually, I must mention here, that this memory about a head is incorrect, as the fine drawing made of it in 1608, clearly shows that there was no head, but that the top part has in fact been broken off. Of course it is possible that the older villagers had preserved memories from their forefathers, but the year 1648 is definitely incorrect.

The fourth report of the statue

This report was published in the *Rheinischer Antiquarius*, a book published in 1739 by an anonymous author. The ruling governor of the county in this time, Landgrave Ernest Leopold (1684-1749)[39] had given orders in 1736-37 for the statue to be excavated, in case there were artifacts underneath. The author of the *Rheinischer Antiquarius*, in his Dedication praised the Landgrave for arranging the recent investigation of the 'flame column' saying,

> ...your Excellency's penetrating intelligence and fine discernment in arranging for the investigation into, and assessment of, culturally significant monuments, an example of which in this regard, immediately comes to mind being the ancient column, which some years ago was discovered at Pfalzfeld, and which in accordance with your Lordship's orders, was excavated. [40]

---

[38] "*Burg Rheinfels*, (Handbook to the castle) R. Engel, St. Goar, 1979.
[39] Appointed by the authority of Frederick 1st, who was also king of Sweden.
[40] Denkwürdigen und nutzlicher **Rheinischer Antiquarius** welcher die wichtigsten und angenehmissten Geographß-Histor- und Politisch Merkwürdigkeiten des ganzen Rhein-Stroms... Frankfurt am Mayn, Erben und Schilling, 1739.

Alte Saule
Rheinfels zu
dem Kirchhof

so ohnweit
Pfaltzfeld auf
Geständen.

Caption reads:
Old column, not
far from (castle)
Rheinfels: in
Pfalzfeld,
standing in the
church grounds.

7 Drawing of statue from 1737

The anonymous author concludes it is also very likely that it is a 'pagan' cult object because,

> the pagan people set up their sacred places deep in forests, and Pfalzfeld had once been located in a dense forest landscape. Furthermore the quire (or 'choir') of the church stood entirely by itself in a circular form, to which the nave of the church has been connected, and this situation by all conjectures suggests that once this site was a pagan temple.

Fortunately, the writer also included a somewhat rough drawing of the statue, which again shows how much taller it originally was. It is now 1.06 metres high, so more than two metres have been broken off the statue since 1608, see illustration 7. Illustration 9 shows the church which was built over the ancient sacred Celtic site, where the statue was originally erected. This carving was intriguing to both Winckelmann and the author of the *Rheinischer Antiquarius*, because it was so striking, and because no-one could identify whom it depicted.

The old book from 1739, in referring to 'pagans', was thinking of the Teutonic tribes people; however the carving is not from the time of the Teutonic tribes (about 100 BC - AD 750) but is ancient Celtic. We now know that it was carved about 500 BC, in the La Tene Celtic era; but in 1737, no-one knew about these Celtic people, who had once occupied most of central Europe. That no-one could identify just what an object of such size and significance depicted, meant that it was continually viewed as a very intriguing object. Illustration 8 shows the covers of the book by this anonymous author and that by Winckelmann.

Consequently, some years after the investigation of 1690, with interest in the mysterious carving remaining high, it had to undergo its first relocation. In 1736, it was removed to the castle Rheinfels, where it was placed in the garden of the Commander of the castle, General-Lieutenant Kutzleben. It appears likely that in this process, it was damaged. Between 1737 and 1938, it would be repeatedly damaged. Paintings reproduced in illustration 10, depict the Rhineland as it was when it was discovered.

8 The first two books to report on the Vidar statue.

9 **The church in Pfalzfeld,** built over the Druidic site. It
was on the boundary of the church yard here, that the
Vidar statue had been originally set up.

10 The beautiful Rhineland of Hesse-Rheinfels, in earlier times.

Above: A vista that reflects the 19th century era of C. Koenen.
(by C.H. Schilbach, 1832)

Below: A scene that invokes the 17th & 18th centuries: the time of
Dilich, Winckelmann, & the Landgraves of Hesse-Rheinfels-
Rotenburg. (by C.G. Schütz, ca. 1770)

In 1805, it was removed to the town of Koblenz, and placed on a black marble pedestal and given an inscription, identifying it as a Roman artwork. It was apparently in the move of 1805 that nearly two metres of its upper part was broken off. Two years later, in 1807, when a new road was opened between St. Goar and Simmern, the statue was placed at the boundary between these two towns.

Later, in 1845, for its protection from the elements, it was moved to the churchyard of St. Goar. But then it was moved from the churchyard to the town square;[41] but not long after this it was taken back to the churchyard. In 1868, another book about the Antiquities of the area mentions its presence in the churchyard wall.[42]

There the statue stayed until shortly after 1928, when it was once again moved; this time back to the castle Rheinfels, but now into a room inside the castle. Finally, in 1938 it was moved permanently into the museum in Bonn. (In 1915, a gypsum cast had been made of it, and this can be seen today in castle Rheinfels.)

How it was understood during all these years can be seen from various reports. In 1848, as it stood in the churchyard of St. Goar, Alexander Grebel reports that,

> It was regarded as "a memory column; a wonder". That expert in antiquities, High Court official, Herr A. Reichensperger, regards the monument as a pre-Christian, Celtic-Gallic statue; which idea appears all the more reasonable, because it came from the vicinity of Pfalzfeld in the hilly "Hunsrück" area, where according to old traditions, once a pagan temple stood.[43]

During the 19th century, the carving was mentioned in several other reports about Antiquities in the area, and, as was the case back in 1608 with W. Dilich, through to the 21st century, the researchers into archaeology and Antiquities were unable to identify just whom this artwork depicts. The 19th century writers generally concluded that it was pre-Teutonic, probably "Gallic" in nature, meaning it was of Celtic origin.

---

[41] Alexander Grebel, Geschichte der Stadt St. Goar, von Alexander Grebel, Carl Sassenroth, St. Goar, 1848.
[42] Ernst Aus'm Weerth, Kunstdenkmäler des Christlichen Mittelalters in dem Rheinlanden.
[43] Ibid., p. 410.

Breakthrough

In 1901, with knowledge of the old Celtic culture developing, a skilled archaeologist and highly regarded researcher in German Antiquities, Constantin Koenen (1854-1929), undertook the most important investigation of the statue. It was then in its location in the wall of the churchyard of St. Goar. His photograph of it there, one winter's day in 1901, gives us a wonderful, evocative image of this 'orphaned' damaged artwork, so significant to its creators, but so misunderstood, so puzzling, to people of modern times; see illustration 11.

He was able to establish its cultural origin as from the La Tene Celtic Age. No other image of Vidar has ever been found, and, as Koenen reports, "it is the most significant Celtic artwork ever found north of the Alps". His words remain true today, despite the recent find of a Vidar-associated carving in the same county (see Appendix Two). Koenen's drawing of the statue is also a very valuable contribution to understanding what it is depicting, see illustration 12. In illustration 13 are portraits of the first researchers or rulers who discovered or made enquiry into this artwork.

Now, before we contemplate what the Druidic initiates wanted to convey (and conceal) by arranging for this large and impressive carving to be set up in one of their sacred sites, we need to know that it is in fact, four-sided; hence Grebel, in 1848, referred to it as "a pyramid or a flame column".[44] See illustration 14, which shows two of its four sides.

One of these two sides shows the face as a younger deity, with the mouth closed and without a beard. The other side however, shows Vidar as an older deity, with a beard, and with his mouth open, indicating that he is now speaking. My sketch, which places these two sides together, and with much of the missing upper parts of the statue restored, is an attempt to present what this carving was originally intended to depict, see illustration 15.

---

[44] Ref. 21, p. 409.

11 The Vidar statue in 1901 at St. Goar
Taken by Constantin Koenen, it is an invaluable record of the
statue's features at that time.

12 The sketch by C. Koenen from 1901, at St. Goar
A skilled and evocative drawing of the mysterious carving.

Above: **Constantin Koenen**, 1901
photograph & drawing & Report.
Above right: **Wilhelm Dilch** 1608,
made the first drawing.
Centre: **Landgrave Ernst**, in 1690
ordered a village enquiry.
Below right: **J. J. Winckelmann**, in
1697, published a report in his
landmark book.
Below left: **Landgrave Ernst
Leopold**, in 1737 excavated and
made enquiry as to its nature.

13 The first people to discover and investigate the statue

Contemplating the statue of Vidar

It is useful to note here again the words of Rudolf Steiner that,

> "a depiction of him was found in the vicinity of Cologne, **of which no-one knows whom it portrays**, but which is nothing other than an image of Vidar."

The very important academic article about this statue by Constantin Koenen in 1901, who took the excellent photograph of it in St. Goar, was published in the *Altertumsfreunde* (*Friends of Antiquity*) journal. His report became the major incident that alerted scholars world-wide to its existence, especially archaeologists and scholars in German and Celtic artifacts. This journal, as of the 1st. Feb. 1901, had some 500 subscribers, of whom 12 were in Berlin, where Rudolf Steiner then lived and where he could have seen the detailed report by Koenen.

Some of these subscribers were major cultural institutions such as the Royal Museum of Berlin (now called the Old Museum). The Director of this museum (Cahn. Frowein) also received his own copy. Other recipients of the report by Koenen were in Cambridge University, and institutions or private persons in Amsterdam, Brussels, Vienna, Budapest, Prague, Rome, Parma (Italy), Cairo, and Baltimore. The publication of his report, just nine years before Rudolf Steiner's lecture in Oslo, justified Rudolf Steiner's comments made there, that it was a striking enigma to scholars {everywhere}, yet "....no-one knows whom it portrays".[45]

The Reconstructed Vidar Carving

We have seen that the statue is four-sided, and comes from the ancient Celtic priests, the Druids. Two of the four sides show the god as a young deity, with a closed mouth. So this represents Vidar in ancient times, prior to taking up his mission; a young silent (not-speaking) deity. The other two sides depict this deity as an older being, shown by a beard, and he has an opened mouth; hence is now speaking. The photograph from 1901 (illustration 11, p. 44) and from recent times, in the Museum, (illustration 14, p. 50) show clearly that the two sides with the bearded figure is longer, and hence the

---

[45] The list of Subscribers is in: *Verzeichnis der Mitglieder im Jahre 1901*, sämmtlicher Mitglieder nach den Wohnorten, p267-69.

lily-form is shorter. Whereas the two sides of the young Vidar have a longer lily-form underneath a shorter face.

The older-looking depiction of Vidar is saying that he is now attempting to actively inspire human beings towards spiritual wisdom and higher consciousness. This combination of young and old countenances is very true to the nature of Vidar as indicated in the Edda and as explained by Rudolf Steiner. A silent god, in ancient times, but who in a later age (which is now) shall begin to speak.

In addition, towering up above him is a series of leaves, amidst some typical Celtic spiral forms. These all tell us that the deity here is (or later will be) exerting his influence from within the ethers. And one reason for the column having four sides could be that the ethers are in fact fourfold: the warmth-ether, the light-ether, the tone- or water-ether, and the life-ether.

We can note here too, that there are no features of the statue which speak of a deity who is fighting a dragon – a prominent feature of the brief references to Vidar in the Edda. As we noted earlier, Rudolf Steiner stated that the artwork would not be recognizably a depiction of Vidar – except to an initiate (or in the modern world, someone who had studied anthroposophy).

After careful inspection of the photographs provided by the Museum, and the various drawings of the statue, 1 could detect that the eyes are closed; as Dilich also depicted in his 1608 drawing. This indicates that they are seeing into the spiritual realm. Rudolf Steiner mentioned the same custom amongst the ancient Greeks; they referred to Homer as blind, but this meant that he was clairvoyant, and thus not primarily focussed on the physical world for his work. This feature in the carving is indicating that it is through the influence of Vidar that those who develop themselves become endowed with some clairvoyance.

On either side of the head, reaching up high above it, are two noticeable forms; these appear to be astral ears. This unusual feature is found in various Celtic artworks. See illustration 16 for examples of other Druidic-Celtic deities or initiates with these large ears. The new clairvoyance will not only be a spiritual seeing, it will also be a spiritual hearing; and this statue is pointing to the new hearing within the ethers for those who in modern times seek spiritual development. This theme of 'spiritual hearing' is an integral part of the great Foundation Stone meditation by Rudolf Steiner. In each of its three main sections, when the three great Rosicrucian maxims are mentioned, the text then says,

> The Spirits hear this
> In east, west, north, south:
> May human beings hear it !

The reference to the four directions is a phrase used by Rudolf Steiner to indicate the *ethereal* cosmos, the universe on an etheric level.[46] This feature of the great verse seems to affirm my conclusion that the four sides of the Vidar statue do allude to the four ethers. In regard to spiritual awakening, there are some demands on modern people seeking spirituality with regard to an inner hearing; there is a need for a conscious awareness of the more subtle experiences that we are allowed to have, in our more sensitive moments. The new clairvoyance commences as delicate points of light in the air, or subtle thoughts (or astral forms), which waft towards the person, on the ethers; and both of these experiences, the visual and the inner audible, are easily ignored.

The decorative feature consisting of leaf forms on the head, includes two such forms on the forehead. These seem to represent the two-petalled 'third eye' or forehead chakra: the organ for spiritual seeing. But in addition to these, the countenance of the Archangel on each side of the statue has some very striking features, incorporating a lily form, which relate to the theme of the Holy Grail. We shall explore those later. Let's now clarify our understanding of how this statue looked originally; at least, up to its broken-off point. My sketch attempts to re-construct its features, which includes the lily shape, up above the head.

This second lily is depicted clearly in the drawing by Dilich in 1608 and again by Koenen in both his drawing and his photograph of 1901. The leaf-forms on the forehead are visible in the photographs made for me by the Museum. There are also two scroll-like swirls which descend from this, to merge with a diamond-shaped formation that points directly to Vidar. To understand what these features are pointing to, we need to engage with Rudolf Steiner's further revelations about Vidar.

---

[46] In a lecture of 13th Nov. 1921, in GA 208, p. 199.

14 The statue in the museum: the old & young or silent and speaking versions of Vidar can be seen here clearly.

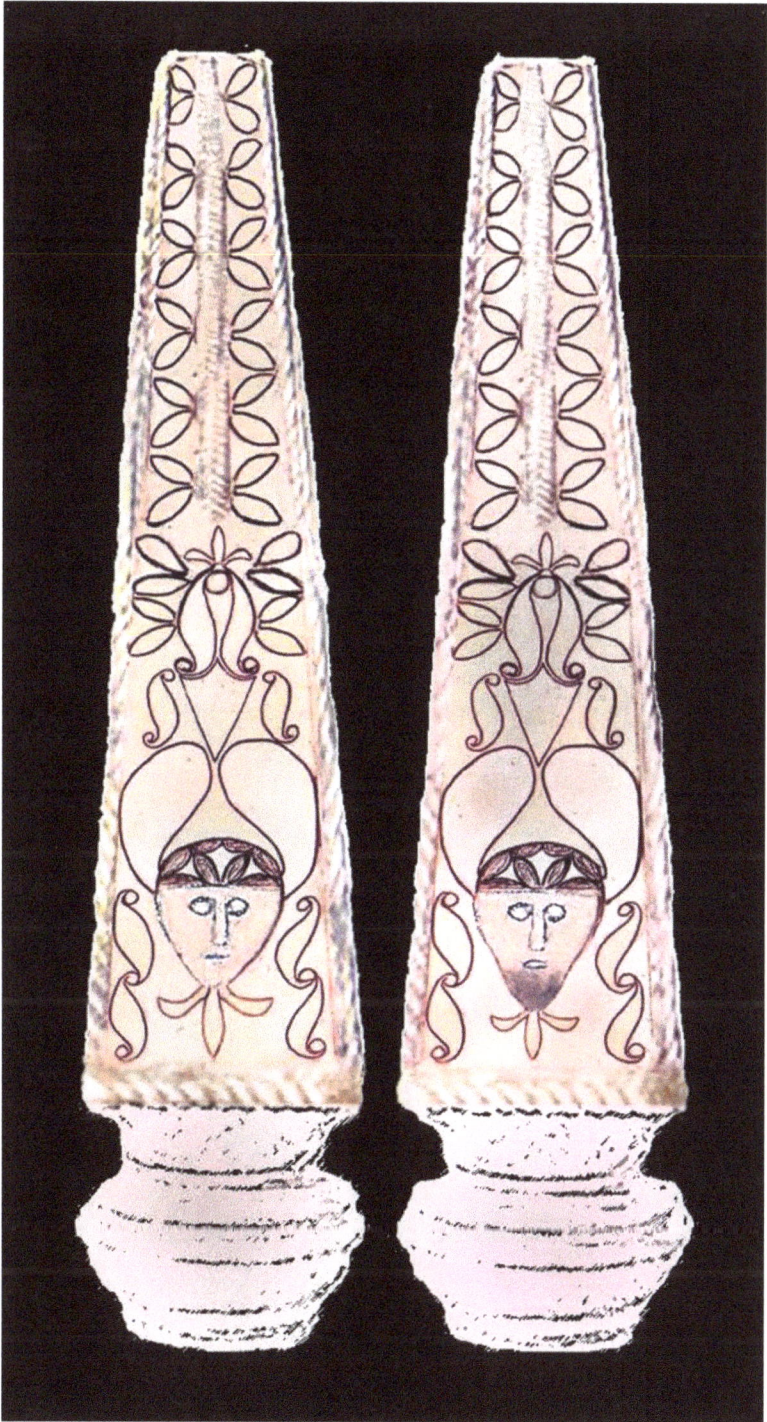

15 Two of the four sides of the reconstructed column
Two sides each depict the mouth closed and no beard; the
other two sides each show the mouth open, and a beard.

16 Examples of astral hearing forms

These six Celtic images, found in central Europe, mainly in Germany, depict deities or initiates.

They date from the same phase of the La Tene Celtic era as the Vidar statue, (about 450-400 BC) except the upper right image which is from the 1st century AD.

Waldalgesheim

To contemplate further revelations about Vidar, takes us into a sacred area of anthroposophy, namely the actual relationship of the individual human soul to the Christ-impulse. This is because Rudolf Steiner revealed indirectly, in lectures given in 1913 and in 1914, that the Archangel Vidar is directly connected to the spiritual renewal of humanity, in an extraordinary way. It was my privilege when researching the nature of this Archangel in the 1980's, to discover that Rudolf Steiner had given veiled indications about what we could call, an 'esoteric virgin birth'. This phrase does not refer to the well-known Biblical theme connected with the birth of Jesus, but to an inner process affecting the astral body. We shall explore this in the next chapter.

Chapter Four

Archangel Vidar, Christ and a 'virgin birth'

We begin to sense more closely the sacred nature and power of this Archangel when we contemplate the words spoken by Rudolf Steiner at the Address he gave in 1913 at the dedication of a branch of the Anthroposophical Society in Bochum, Germany, whose members decided it should be called the "Vidar branch". During his speech he referred many times to Jesus Christ. His address is primarily about the, at times turbulent activity of earthly nature spirits and other beings in the seasonal cycle, in contrast to the inner harmony of the sun.

He then makes reference to the spiritual sun, and points out that St. Luke's gospel presents us with the nativity of Jesus as the one divine or 'un-fallen' human being who becomes the vessel of Christ. Rudolf Steiner refers to him as the "Nathan Jesus" soul, from the name of one of his ancestors, a son of King David. [47]

It is to this uniquely divine soul, when he was 29 years old, that the cosmic Christ descended, at the Baptism in the Jordan River. Once this event occurred, then the Saviour of humanity, Jesus Christ, came into being. The spiritual union of these two was deepened and made eternal by the Crucifixion and Resurrection in AD 33. Towards the end of this Address he says,

> Our friends here wish to dedicate their branch to the name of **that god** who in the north is acknowledged as the god who wishes to bring back to aging mankind, rejuvenating forces: spiritual child-hood forces. This is the god to whom the Nordic souls are directly referring when they wish to speak of that, which arising from Christ Jesus, brings us human beings new tidings of a rejuvenation.[48]

The conclusion is inescapable here that, since his conversion, Vidar exerts his influence in very close proximity to Christ Jesus. Let's consider again the words given earlier,

---

[47] This title clearly refers to Jesus of Luke's Gospel, and differentiates him from Jesus in St. Matthew's Gospel, whose genealogy identifies him as a descendant of Solomon.

[48] GA 150, lecture, 21st Dec. 1913.

Teutonic mythology knows that the etheric form exists in which shall be embodied that which we are destined to see again – Christ, in an etheric form. He alone shall succeed in banishing the dark and impure clairvoyant powers which would confuse mankind if Odhin were not to succeed in overcoming the Fenris Wolf {which symbolizes the atavistic clairvoyance}. Vidar, who has been silent until now, shall overcome the Fenris Wolf.

These words can easily lead one to question whether Vidar and Christ are the same being. It is clear that they are not the same being, but it is also clear that this Archangel's activity is merged in some way with the Christ being. And secondly, as his statue shows, his field of activity is in the ethers. Let's now consider the words of Rudolf Steiner which we placed at the front of the book,

> After the mystery of Golgotha, humanity must strive to make this experience of an en-souled, spiritualized nature {thus the seasonal cycle with its various nature spirits} constitute the following of Christ...for the nature spirits can all be seen in the following of Christ, but without Him they cannot be seen. This however, is indicated precisely here {in Norway} in that the people here were informed about this – that from out of the host of ancient spirit-beings, Vidar shall again appear, in a new form...

We experience again a strongly implied closeness of the Archangel and the Saviour. But now we can also see that this lecture in Bochum has been moving around the themes occurring in the above words: nature sprites, the seasonal cycle, becoming aware of the seasonal cycle as a {new, esoteric} Christian activity.[49]

In essence, these two lecture extracts are revealing that Vidar plays a crucial role in the phenomenon of people experiencing the Reappearing of Jesus Christ in the ethers, and awakening to the awareness of the ethers, through a new clairvoyance. This same awakening can also assist people to develop new festivals; festivals which are seasonally related, but esoterically Christian. To commence our journey into this special theme, we start with these words of Rudolf Steiner,

---

[49] See my book, *"Living a Spiritual Year: seasonal festivals in northern and southern hemispheres,* for a full presentation of this theme.

(quotation marks shall be used from now on, to clearly identify quotes from Rudolf Steiner),

> "Anthroposophy is something which shines forth from mankind, it blossoms forth from the finest forces of humanity; thus it will be something which renews and revivifies humanity's earthly existence".[50]

Such words naturally raise the question, how do we attain to "the finest forces of humanity"? The answer is revealed, and to some extent concealed, in the final lecture Rudolf Steiner gave in the cycle about the Gospel of St. Luke. He begins to speak about something especially mysterious and linked to the "finest forces of humanity". He informed his audience that,

> "As every person enters into incarnation, something is added to that person which does not arise from the process of conception, but which comes from the spiritual worlds....something is streamed into the person's ego, and it can be ennobled through the Christ-impulse.
>
> This process is connected with the Mystery of Golgotha, because prior to that event, it did not happen. Thus every person has a "virgin birth"; something is given to him which is additional to that produced by the conception process and this which is so given, must be gradually developed and ennobled by assimilating the Christ-impulse {in life after life}."

Later in the lecture he adds,

> "This new element can be gravely impaired if a person is entirely given over to materialistic thought. But it can be sublimated if he lets his being be suffused by the warmth issuing from the Christ-impulse; he then can bring this into ever higher forms in succeeding incarnations.
>
> People can destroy this additional element if they turn away from the Christ-impulse, but they can nurture and develop it, if they receive into themselves what streams from the Christ-impulse."

---

[50] GA 211, lecture, 26th Mar. 1922.

We need to be clear that the "additional element" in the human being's soul is called 'virginal', meaning that it is not derived from the parental physical, etheric or astral qualities. It is essential that one reads this lecture, as giving only a summary of it can not properly convey the profound revelation offered there. But the next words of Rudolf Steiner take us substantially towards intuiting the mystery of Vidar. He reveals that this additional, 'virginal' element in the soul is not wholly un-connected to us,

> "The ethical spirituality of the infant is a last echo, a ray, of this virginal part of man's being..."

In the little infant and toddler, there is present an exquisite spiritual quality; this manifests as a natural capacity for experiencing wonder and awe, and a feeling of reverence before the sacred.

It is the essence of the lectures on the Gospel of St. Luke, that there was but one human soul who did not enter into the 'Fall of Man'. That is, the process which occurred some millions of years ago wherein human beings were impelled by the influence of Lucifer and Ahriman to develop flesh bodies and enter into the consciousness of the physical world, where the earthly ego, with its lower self, could develop. [51]

There was one soul who did not become influenced by Lucifer and Ahriman, and who consequently never entered into the journey of many lifetimes on the Earth. That one soul is Jesus, whose Nativity is described in Luke's Gospel. This is the soul whom Rudolf Steiner described as uniquely capable of manifesting all the Love that a human being can ever attain. At this point, we need to note significant words from a different lecture cycle, which closely refers to the influence of Vidar, as a spiritual activity, exerting itself in close inter-connectedness with that of Christ. He tells his audience that we human beings cannot gain awareness of the spirit through our own unaided activity towards spirituality;

> "...something has had to stream into our very being, from outside us, something which comes from the spiritual worlds, and which signifies a renewal, a resurrection, a new rejuvenation of us; of that which

---

[51] The 'Fall of Man' occurred in mid-Lemurian times, some time after the moon was cast out of the Earth, which was 18 million years ago.

has brought humanity into being, which had thereafter withdrawn into the depths of our consciousness."[52]

To gradually realize what these words are pointing towards, we need to remind ourselves that already long ago, Jesus had an inherent affinity to the cosmic Christ, and as a result of this, whilst humanity was struggling in life after life on a darkening Earth, there occurred what Rudolf Steiner calls the three "pre-steps to the Mystery of Golgotha". It is important to read the lectures in which he describes what this term means. Here we can just briefly report what is involved here.

Rudolf Steiner's words on this theme revealed a profoundly moving and inspiring situation, in which three deeds were undertaken by Jesus, within as it were, the wings of an Angel and also an Archangel who are in the presence of the Cosmic Christ. The essential points on this theme from his lectures on "*The Pre-earthly Deeds of Christ*" are these:[53]

First redeeming event:
The first event occurred millions of years ago in the Lemurian Age, soon after the first dawning of a rudimentary ego-capacity in humanity. The twelve-fold zodiacal powers which were forming the body, and also, through our sun-sign, were forming the foundation of the ego-sense, became subject to Ahrimanic and Luciferic influences. These were disturbing the 12 senses of the human being, with the result that these were threatened with an inherent ego-centric quality. This meant that intense desires and emotive reactions would have assaulted the human being as the senses functioned.

If a colour were unpleasant, the antipathy would have been so potent that the person would have been hurled away, screaming, from the object; the soul would feel as if burning fiercely by the pain. But if another coloured object was experienced as pleasant, the other dynamic would have happened: human beings would have thrown themselves in utter desire upon it, now consumed by an inner fire, a burning desire.

The anguish arising in humanity, as this situation approached, rose up to the soul of Jesus, who was in the

---

[52] GA 129, *Wonders of the World, Ordeals of the Soul, Revelations of the Spirit*, lecture, 25th Aug. 1911, p. 178 (German edition).
[53] See the single lecture: "*The Pre-earthly Deeds of Christ*, 7th March 1914, or the entire book of lectures on this subject (GA no. 152).

higher Devachanic realms. As He became filled with compassion for humanity, he moved into the presence of the sublime Sun-God, Christ. Christ then permeated his being, and these combined forces from the Christ-permeated, divine Jesus soul streamed down upon the earth, permeating the sense-system of humanity, and this allowed the 12 senses to develop as objective organs of perception.

Second redeeming event:
Later on, in early Atlantean times, a similar danger occurred with the developing seven life-organs which in themselves are a reflection of the seven planets, (the lungs, liver, kidneys, heart, gall and so on). The internal consciousness qualities that these vital organs induce in us, as an undercurrent sustaining our soul-life, was threatened with a wild, self-centredness. Consequently the lungs themselves would have sucked in the air with fierce passion, or clammed up and moved the person away from air they did not like.

Again the anguish of this situation, of a situation which started to become possible, was perceived by He who would later be known as Jesus of Nazareth. He who again in His infinite compassion drew the Cosmic Christ near to Himself, and once again became permeated by divine healing forces. This situation allowed these forces to descend into the earthly sphere, bringing an end to this possible situation.

Third redeeming event:
It was towards the end of the Atlantean age, as individualism was slowly and subtly arising, that individual thinking appeared (very faintly). At this time, a third danger arose from the increasing power of the Ahrimanic and Luciferic forces in the earthly sphere. Now the triune consciousness of the soul, that is, thinking, emotion and will, were threatened with an astral force which would undermine coordinated mental activity. If disturbed mental qualities, even insanity, were to be avoided, then these three qualities must be harmoniously interrelated with each other.

The human being would have reacted with sheer emotive force, without allowing the logical mind to advise on the situation, or carried out will-impulses, even if the emotions were against this. Again, Jesus, perceiving this, drew near to the great source of humanity's inner being, the highest of the Elohim, or the sun god Christ, and once more divine forces permeated his soul, and these then emanated downwards, entering into the Earth sphere, permeating the planet's aura.

In this context, the Mystery of Golgotha, was a fourth such redeeming and helping undertaken by Jesus as permeated by the great Sun-god. In his various lectures on this theme Rudolf Steiner revealed that Jesus was assisted by a special Angel and the Archangel Michael. Awareness of this **third** event was attained by those in the Mysteries, founded after the end of Atlantis, and the myth of the Archangel Michael, slaying the dragon, was the outcome of this awareness.

Now, with awareness of this context, those striking words we quoted just before noting the three pre-steps to the Golgotha event, begin to unveil their meaning. In that lecture Rudolf Steiner is referring to the achieving of a spiritual consciousness (even clairvoyance). It is especially the words, *"something has had to stream into our very being, from outside us, something which comes from the spiritual worlds..."* that suggest a continuation of the help from the Christ-impulse. In the Gospel of St. Luke cycle, it is exactly this additional help that Rudolf Steiner is discreetly referring to.

He reveals this to his audience saying,

> ...these were significant deeds, made possible only by the assistance given by Christ, active within the being of Jesus, who at that time was an Angelic being. For, this being had to actually connect himself with the 'Dragon-nature'; he had to take on, as it were, the form of the Dragon, in order to hold off the Dragon from the souls of people. He had to work from within the Dragon, so that it was ennobled and brought out of chaos, and into a kind of harmony. The training or taming of the Dragon **is the further task of the being** {Jesus Christ, as He is now called}.

It appears from the brief lecture notes that "this being" refers to Jesus Christ (as He is now called) and the Archangel Michael being active together, in a process in which the sun god Christ is also present. But what we need to note here especially, is that Jesus himself, until he became the immensely empowered Saviour, with an eternal ego or higher self, was the unfallen, primal 'child of mankind'. For he had not been drawn into the Fall of Man, but remained divine.

Rudolf Steiner was permitted through his profound spirituality to behold the life of Jesus which is imprinted in the Akashic Record. He reports that when Jesus was incarnated, just shortly before he walked to the Jordan River for his baptism, the culminating experience of his life so far, occurred. This experience concerned the problem of how to help humanity find an inner renewal. Over some years, Jesus had beheld the strong influence that Lucifer and Ahriman had achieved over human beings. He could see that humanity was in dire need of being given a rejuvenation, for the age-old spiritual reservoir of light in the astral and etheric bodies had all but disappeared. His soul was deeply grappling with this urgent need facing humanity.

His most urgent life-question was: how can humanity be rejuvenated, actually? From what source can this flow forth? It was, Rudolf Steiner reports, the impact of this soul-anguish that actually impelled Jesus to walk towards the Jordan, there to become the vessel of the cosmic Christ, and thus the archetype of the spiritually perfect, or indeed 'rejuvenated' human being. For it was he himself, who would be his answer. Once he became permeated by the great sun god Christ, he would be the source of humanity's spiritual rebirth.

These perspectives are essential to grasp the following words from Rudolf Steiner about the 'virgin birth', from his last lecture in the Gospel of St. Luke cycle,

> "The 'virginal part' of man is the last remnant of man's being, which has undergone evolution in the Saturn, Sun and Moon Aeons, and which today constitutes the 'unconscious part' of man's being. This part consequently, has not undergone being subject to Luciferic influences...the 'unconscious part' of man's being is his childhood qualities. That is, the ethical virtues present in the little child: this is a ray of the 'virginal part' of man's being."

> "The macrocosmic 'fountain' of this childhood radiance is today, and ever since the Mystery of Golgotha, streaming into the human being. This in-streaming childhood virtuous spirituality must, so far as the human being is concerned, be united with the echo of itself that is still present in every human being."

And then Rudolf Steiner reveals the sacredness of the inner link between the human soul and Christ, on this deep level. He is pointing to the being-ness of Jesus Christ (or "Christ Jesus"), saying that this can offer the pathway to spiritual redemption,

> "...the conjoining of the primal, unfallen spiritual part of our nature, to the faintly present echo of itself, in us, must re-invigorate this residual echo and thus renew the rest of the human soul."

And in this sacred process, flowing from the Saviour, the Archangel Vidar is assisting, as the words spoken at the dedication of the Bochum branch of the Society was indicating,

> "Our friends here wish to dedicate their branch to the name of **that god** who in the north is acknowledged as the god who wishes to bring back to aging mankind, rejuvenating forces: **spiritual child-hood forces**. This is the god to whom the Nordic souls are directly referring when they wish to speak of that, which **arising from Christ Jesus**, brings us human beings new tidings of **a rejuvenation**."   (Emphasis mine, A.A.)

So the way to high spirituality is by transforming the spirituality, glowing all unconsciously in the young child. Rudolf Steiner calls this the "spiritual childhood forces". At this point we need to think of those words from Rudolf Steiner given in the lecture of 1911,

> "...something has had to stream into our very being, from outside us, something which comes from the spiritual worlds, and which signifies a resurrection, a rejuvenation of us..."

Just before he spoke this, he told his audience a deep truth which relates to the 'virgin birth' Mystery, but also to the new clairvoyance, associated with Vidar,

> "There is only one thing in Earth-evolution through which something new, a new element of clairvoyance, which is also however a new element of human activity, and of the human mind and feelings, permeated by hidden forces, can enter us."

The rest of the lecture makes it clear that it is the 'virgin birth' Christ-influences that he is referring to. These words also point directly to the involvement, in the rejuvenation of humanity of Vidar; for in Oslo, he is also described as the divine being "who is to bring about the new clairvoyance".

So the implication of all the above statements from Rudolf Steiner are that, as a result of the events of Golgotha, we human beings have a subtle ray of spiritual light – the essence of the True, the Good and the Beautiful – given to us, as we prepare to incarnate. This light derives from Christ Jesus, who is the great archetype of the redeemed human being. Also, the implication here is, that the Archangel Vidar is assisting Christ Jesus to bring this light into the child as it descends for rebirth. But it is also clearly indicated that Vidar is helping those people, who as adults seek spirituality, to nurture and develop this light. If this process occurs sufficiently strongly, then the new clairvoyance arises.

The following words from Rudolf Steiner, spoken about eight months after indicating the secrets of the great Archangel Vidar in Oslo, sum up what we have now learnt about the way that the human soul attains to spirituality, or becomes as it were, a 'Christ-permeated' person, through the 'virgin birth',

> "We have to permeate ourselves with the transformation of that which lives in us in early childhood: then is the Christ in us."[54]

This is the reason that the anthroposophical path to self-initiation starts with the requirement to nurture the 'Four Moods'. That is, to bring back to life in one's soul, the capacity for experiencing awe, to feel wonder, to have reverence for all that is holy and beautiful; and lastly to be capable of devotion.[55] The term 'devotion' here means to be able to exercise one's will for a purpose that is not self-centred.

These contemplations appear to show why it is, that the Druidic initiates arranged for the Vidar statue to have both young and old countenances carved into it.

The Lily and the Rose
Bearing in mind what we discovered regarding the role of Vidar in connection with the ongoing influence of Christ, in seeking to help redeem humanity, the image of a lily and roses comes to mind. The Nativity story in St. Luke's Gospel could be viewed as proclaiming a lily, meaning a divine soul,

---

[54] GA 127, lecture, 25th Feb. 1911, p. 97.
[55] For a comprehensive guide to the meditative path, see my, *The Way to the Sacred.*

untainted by the earth, descending down to Bethlehem, amidst the rejoicing of the Angels. The Nativity story in St. Matthew's Gospel would then be about a rose, a soul who has gathered many experiences through engaging with earthly life, and has thereby worked his way to a resplendent purity and wisdom. It is the spiritual union of these two qualities that came together in Jesus.

And now, whenever a child is about to be born, the Angels gaze down on it, beholding a glowing radiance in the child's aura. This is caused by a lily-like radiance coming into being and finding a place within a faint after-echo of itself, present in the child's aura. This contrasts to the darker red tones of earthly yearnings and desires. The Angels are wondering, shall the lily-like radiance grow stronger through this earthly lifetime, or shall it weaken? Can this lily-like glow so permeate and empower the after-echo of itself, that a more gentle, more noble tone of red suffuses the bloodstream?

The implication of Rudolf Steiner's words about Vidar is that this Archangel helps to convey the 'spiritual childhood forces' into the aura of each human being as they prepare for birth.

This role of Vidar also flows naturally over into a holy activity which assists people seeking a high spirituality, to move towards the Holy Grail mysteries.

Chapter Five

Vidar, Christ and the Holy Grail

The medieval Holy Grail legends, in their fascinating and inspiring narratives, present several different definitions of this especially sacred theme. In the various legends, the Grail can be an actual cup used at the Last Supper, or an emerald stone, or the physical blood of Jesus (a small amount of this preserved in a cup), or a mysterious chalice, and yet also a kind of healing force and a mysterious nourishment.

You can read another view of the Grail in my book on Rudolf Steiner's great Rosicrucian painting, *Rudolf Steiner's esoteric Christianity in the Grail painting by Anna May*. The Grail legends present many different views of this theme, but, they are texts designed to uplift and inspire the wider community, so they all refrain from actually defining which is meant esoterically, by 'the Holy Grail'. The actual esoteric secret of the Grail was only unveiled in the life's work of Rudolf Steiner. Hence in the medieval books, the Holy Grail is a mysterious and enticing topic, imbued with a sacredness, but in many respects remaining unclear.

The Holy Grail is such a veiled topic because it is the most sacred of all spiritual mysteries. Some aspects of the most sacred spiritual truths may have to remain a mystery, until one unveils it for oneself, through a meditative engagement with the legends and Rudolf Steiner's indications.

If we consider a few brief points about this theme from the book, "*Parzival*" by Wolfram von Eschenbach, we can detect the level of initiation wisdom behind it. In Book Eleven, Eschenbach refers to an intense and desperate fight that Sir Gawain has to wage with a fierce lion, whilst in his bed. Such an account, which places a battle occurring in the bed, can only derive from initiation knowledge; it refers to the core element of the Holy Grail. That is, the final stage of conquering the sex urge, which starts by overcoming the bull forces (of sensual desire) in the astral body, and finishes with overcoming the lion forces (of ingrained, pre-dispositional tendencies) in the etheric body. Once this stage is reached, then the Spirit-self is attained, together with the beginning of the glorious Life-Spirit. As such the Holy Grail is a theme that opposing spirit powers would like to have disappear from modern awareness, and effort has been made in this direction.[56]

Firstly, with regard to the Vidar statue, we note that a lily shape is placed on the statue, at the throat area. Very significantly however, it is upside down. But also, as illustration 17 shows, there is a second lily-form on the statue, up above the head of Vidar; this one is upright. As I mentioned earlier, although this second higher lily form is no longer to be seen on the original statue owing to the amount of damage done to it since 1901, it is clearly present in the photograph by Koenen and in earlier drawings.

This lily form became known as a *fleur-de-lis* in France, and this symbol has been used (the right way up) for different purposes by various cultures throughout history. It is significant that it occurs in medieval Grail legends as a symbol of the Grail. So what do these two symbols mean here, on an ancient, Celtic, pre-Christian statue? Was there some equivalent to the Grail, prior to the coming of Christ ?

Before we explore this question, we need to note Rudolf Steiner's striking words about Vidar in this connection. We mentioned earlier that there are two occasions in which Vidar actually speaks some words. The first occasion is noted in the Edda, and occurred long ago; it was when Loki demanded access to humanity, that is, to have a seat at the table of the Gods. The second occasion comes from Rudolf Steiner, and is one of those very rare times when he reveals his interaction with spirit beings in higher realms. It must have been with some astonishment that his audience heard that, in his quest to understand the Holy Grail, (obviously more deeply than he already understood it), Rudolf Steiner entered into a dialogue with an Archangelic being: the Archangel Vidar.

He reveals this in a lecture in Leipzig, on 1st January 1914, in a lecture cycle called *Christ and the Spiritual world: the Search for the Holy Grail.*[57] He reports that, some years ago,

---

[56] False interpretations that have an element of blasphemy against Jesus Christ are to be expected in the age which is being drawn towards ahrimanic 'ideals'.

[57] The notes of these lectures are very poor, sections of text are missing, so the book is hard to read.

"I did not quite know how to proceed, when on one occasion, I asked the Norwegian Folk-spirit, the Nordic Folk-Spirit, about Parsifal, and this being said:

"Learn to understand the expression which *through my power* has flowed into the Nordic Parsifal saga –

'Ganganda greida' " : which means something like, the 'circulating nourishment'." *

(* or, 'moving-around provisions for journeying')

We realize firstly, with some surprise, that Rudolf Steiner was seeking help from the Archangel Vidar in his own quest to further understand the Grail. We shall explore why this happened, and what the unusual expression really means. But one further point to note of relevance here in the account by Eschenbach, is that Sir Gawain is identified as a Norwegian Grail knight.[58] And of course it is Sir Gawain who comes closest to succeeding in the search for the Grail, after Parzival himself. There are indications here, that Vidar has an important link to the deep aspects of the Holy Grail.

So what is the connection of Vidar to the Holy Grail? This connection is indicated by the lily symbol which is placed upside down, on all the four sides of the Vidar statue. This feature is a sign of deep initiation knowledge, as we shall soon see. That the second, upper symbol is placed close to the long area of leaves is indicating the etheric realm. Two curved forms also lead down from this to an arrow-head formation, which is pointing directly to Vidar. What do these features point to ?

---

[58] Wolfram von Eschenbach, Parzival, Book 13, p. 342. (Vintage bks.).

17 **The features on and around the head of Vidar**
Though no longer visible today, the two lily-forms are
clearly seen in the older images, as is the arrow-like form
that points toward Vidar from below the upper lily form.

Why is it significant that an upside-down lily is placed at the throat area of the face? Because this is precisely where the Grail centre in the human being – in the etheric body – is located. What does this mean ? The answer is found in an extraordinary Holy Grail lecture by Rudolf Steiner, during which he revealed profound esoteric truths about the spiritualization process of the human being. The lecture is called the *Etherisation of the Blood*, and to fully grasp this veiled aspect of the Grail, one needs to read the lecture in full.

In this lecture he speaks of how,

> "certain rays of {spiritual} light are to be seen streaming constantly from the heart towards the head... there they move around the gland known as the pineal gland. These streamings {of spiritual energy} come into existence because human blood, which is a physical substance {but permeated intensely with astral and etheric forces} is continually transforming itself into etheric energy. In the region of the heart there is a continual transformation of the blood into this tenuous etheric 'substance'. This etheric energy-substance streams upwards, towards the head, and glimmers around the pineal gland...this process is the 'etherization of the blood'. But moreover, the seer is also able to see a continual streaming from outside the human being, into the brain..."

A few minutes later, he then reveals now these dynamics are occurring within the reality of the Earth as a planet now permeated by the cosmic Christ, and in which also lives Jesus Christ as the archetype of the future spiritualized human being,

> "Just as in the region to the heart, blood is being continually transformed into etheric substance, a similar process occurs in the macrocosm. We understand this when we turn our attention to the Mystery of Golgotha – to the moment when the blood flowed from the wounds of the Redeemer. But this blood must not be regarded as chemical substance, but {on its astral and etheric levels} it is something quite exceptional as a result of all the spirituality which is in the nature of Jesus of Nazareth."

"When this flowed from his wounds, a 'substance' was imparted to the Earth, which through the Earth uniting with it, constituted an event of the greatest possible significance for all future ages of the Earth – and it could take place only once. What became of this blood {its astral-etheric energies} ? Nothing different from what takes place in the heart of man."

"In the course of Earth's evolving, this blood passes through a process of etherisation. And just as our blood as an etheric energy streams upwards from the heart, likewise, since the Mystery of Golgotha, the etherised blood of Christ Jesus has been present in the ether-body of the Earth. This fact is important."

"....since the Mystery of Golgotha there has always been the possibility for the etherized blood of Christ to circulate along in unison with the etheric 'streamings' that flow inside a human being, from below upwards {towards the head}."

"Because the etherised blood of Jesus of Nazareth is present in the Earth's ether-body, it accompanies the etherised human being's blood streaming upwards from the heart towards the brain...hence the human {etherized} blood-stream unites with the {etherized} blood-stream of Jesus Christ. But such a union of these two streams can however only come about if the human being is able to unfold a correct {inner} understanding of what the Christ-impulse is."

These inspired words, together with what Rudolf Steiner was told by the great Archangel Vidar, takes the student of anthroposophy to the very deepest secrets of the Holy Grail, and the connection of this to Jesus Christ. As we noted above, Rudolf Steiner was told by Vidar to contemplate the fact that an old Norwegian expression, "**Ganganda greida**" was placed in the Norwegian translation of a primary saga of the Holy Grail. Rudolf Steiner then tells his audience that it means something like 'circulating nourishment'; see illustration 18 for an extract from this rare Norwegian text. The implication of what Rudolf Steiner was told is firstly, that in the Middle Ages, a spiritually advanced Norwegian person was inspired to translate a key text about the Holy Grail ("Perseval" by Chretien de Troyes) to make it available to the people of Vidar, so to speak. In the Middle Ages, the term 'Scandinavia' did not yet exist; instead there were the 'northern German

18 The medieval Old Norwegian Riddara Saga

The cover page and a page with the expression ganganda greida .

RIDDARASÖGUR

PARCEVALS SAGA   VALVERS PÁTTR

IVENTS SAGA   MIRMANS SAGA

ZUM ERSTEN MAL HERAUSGEGEBEN

UND MIT EINER LITERARHISTORISCHEN EINLEITUNG
VERSEHEN

VON

Dr. EUGEN KÖLBING.

STRASSBURG,
KARL J. TRÜBNER,
LONDON,
TRÜBNER & CO.
1872.

peoples' who spoke, or could read, either Old West Scandinavian or Old East Scandinavian. The Grail saga was translated into Old Norwegian, which was understood very widely; Norway ruled over Iceland, Greenland, and some outlying Scottish islands. So Norwegian was also understood then in most of what we now call Scandinavia today. The Danish and Swedish languages had recently emerged from the Old East Scandinavian language, but Old Norwegian was still widely understood by the Nordic people (Norway and Denmark had been in effect one country until 1814).

Secondly, it was during this translation work that the unknown person was inspired by Vidar to provide a Norwegian definition of the word "Grail". When, in the French Grail story by de Troyes, it is said, "...the maid entered carrying the Grail", the Norwegian *Riddarasage* repeats this and then says, "but, we can call it the *circulating nourishment* ". ("Ganganda greida")

This definition provides initiatory understanding of what the Holy Grail really is, at its deepest level. For the Old Norwegian expression, through the inspiration of Vidar, is pointing to the presence, within the spiritualized etheric forces that permeated the blood of the truly spiritual person. These are the holy etheric energies from Christ Jesus himself, circulating within the etheric body of the human being. These spiritualized etheric streams provide the very basis, or 'nourishment' of the inner being of that spiritual person in whom the Spirit-self has developed. It is in such a person that whom the Grail forces are arising; and it is these forces which invoke the Life-spirit.

Now to link these profound truths to the statue of Vidar, we only need to know that these Life-spirit etheric forces sanctified by the indwelling presence of divine etheric forces from the Saviour, accumulate in an upside-down chalice form, which exists within the human being's etheric body, at the area of the throat. That this is the case was revealed by Rudolf Steiner in lectures given at a major international conference in Munich in 1907. He spoke about seven extraordinary artworks which he had arranged to be painted from his own designs, and placed in the conference hall. These are called the Apocalyptic seals. It is the seventh of these which is so striking and inspiring, and which represents the Holy Grail, see illustration 19.

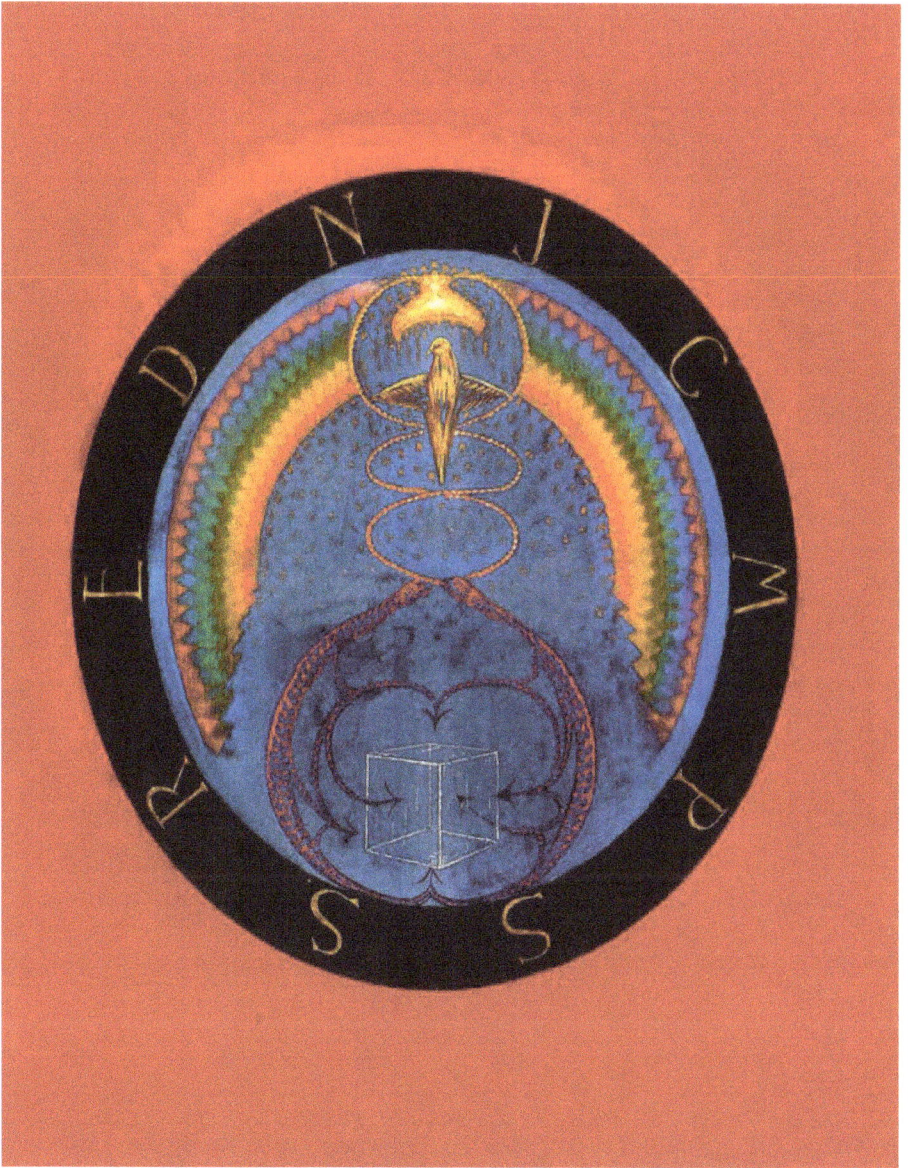

19 The Holy Grail seal from Rudolf Steiner, 1907
The dove is rising up into the etheric chalice at the throat area:
this is the Holy Grail, in its deepest sense.

The term 'seals' here means prominent and empowered astral images, existing in the astral realm. Here in this seal we see many profound and striking features. The feature that is most relevant to the Vidar statue is that the dove, representing the arising Grail etheric energies, is rising up, to enter an upside-down chalice form: the Grail centre in the throat area of the human being. The upside-down chalice form is a more esoteric and detailed way to depict what an upside-down lily form is intended to represent. It is very worthwhile to contemplate this highly esoteric image; see Appendix Five.

The statue of Vidar appears to be indicating, from the ancient Druidic initiation wisdom, that the modern seeker after true spirituality, or self-initiation, needs to make themselves "into a son or daughter of Odhin"; that is, into 'a Vidar person'. This means, a person in whose soul the influences of this Christ-associated archangel can arise. We are accustomed from a knowledge of anthroposophy to accept that one can be a 'Michaelic' person; that is a person whose thinking can grasp concepts that are clear, yet embodying spiritual truths.

In addition, it is now clear that one can also be a 'Vidar-like' person; that is someone in whom the deep purity of the astral body has allowed the etheric body to start to become spiritualized and hence accumulate the Grail ethers. Such a person has the Grail centre in their etheric body, becoming en-filled with the Grail ethers, but the source of this Grail light is a source beyond oneself, in the ethers, just like the second lily-form above the head of Vidar. This source is, as we now know, the divine etheric energies arising from Jesus Christ, present in the Earth's ether aura.

The implication of the features of the statue carved by the Druids, is that the sacred Grail light from Christ Jesus, which merges with the spiritualizing etheric energies of the spiritual seeker, **is mediated into her or his aura with the assistance of the great Archangel Vidar**. This is a higher form of the Virgin Birth process, which we contemplated earlier.

The Druids and the chakras
The question can arise, did the Druids know about this potential reservoir for the Grail energies in ancient times? To identify a specific equivalent to the Grail centre is difficult, but it is probable that anthroposophical wisdom would affirm that, because earlier initiates gained an inner attunement to Christ by accessing the Christ-reality in the sun-sphere.

Celtic literature does refer to a magic cauldron which provides nutrition to the initiates; this appears to have some resemblance to the idea of the Holy Grail. But to know about this Grail centre, the Druids would also need to have some knowledge of the chakras, since the Grail centre is, in some ways, a special additional chakra-like centre. The chakras, of course, are vortices in the astral (and etheric) body which become organs of perception for the initiates; they are what make clairvoyance possible. Is there any evidence that the Druids had knowledge of the chakras? Yes, there is.

Ancient Druidic knowledge of the chakras
In Denmark, in 1891 in a locality known as Gundestrup, a Druid 'magic cauldron' (that is, an initiatory cauldron) was found; it is known as the Gundestrup cauldron. It is made of 97% pure silver, and dates from about 100 BC, or roughly 400 years later than the Vidar statue. It is made of panels which contain esoteric depictions of the process of becoming initiated, which of course means achieving clairvoyance.

But for clairvoyance to occur, it is required that the chakras are brought into a condition of actual spinning or turning. We cannot go into the details of all the panels in this cauldron, but illustration 20 shows a panel of the cauldron, depicting exactly the effort of a Druid acolyte to get their throat chakra spinning. The deity depicted is the spirit of the planet Mars, and the various animal forms depicted indicate the challenge of overcoming the lower astral tendencies.

But what is so striking here is the providing of a small handle, for the acolyte to grasp the wheel and to make sure it spins around – a very clear statement about 'getting the chakra to spin'. This expression means that the chakra is now activated, is no longer dormant, but is actively bringing about perception of higher realities.

20 A panel from the Gundestrup Cauldron: Druidic initiation wisdom

This panel depicts the effort that has to be made specifically to get the throat chakra spinning.

Appendix One: Unveiling the secret of Vidar's shoe

In illustration 1 is a depiction of Vidar putting his foot into the mouth of the Fenris Wolf, from the 10th century column in Gosforth, England. We noted earlier that one of the characteristics of Vidar is that he has a remarkable shoe, which he uses in his battle against the Fenris Wolf,

> Vidar then approaches the wolf and places his shoe upon the wolf's lower jaw. On this foot he has that shoe which is constantly being formed from the scraps of leather which people cast away from their shoes, as they are being made; especially from the toes and heels. Therefore everyone should cast away those scraps, who is concerned with helping the gods.

We have also noted that Vidar is described by Rudolf Steiner as bestowing the new clairvoyance, and conquering the old atavistic psychic ability,

> "...the new spiritual research {Anthroposophy} will re-establish the power of Vidar, who shall banish from the hearts and minds of people all the dark, confusing relics of the old clairvoyance and shall awaken in the human soul the new clairvoyance that is gradually unfolding."

This theme of Vidar's shoe has remained an enigma amongst students of anthroposophy. We can however now solve the initiatory truth that the Druidic initiates wanted to convey in the myth about Vidar and the shoe. To do this, we need to understand some dynamics affecting the etheric body which Rudolf Steiner especially revealed, without mentioning the theme of Vidar.

The etheric body
The cosmic ether is like a sea around the Earth, and it is into this enveloping field of ether that astral energies come streaming in. These astral energies or 'music of the spheres.' resonate within the Earth's ether aura. The Earth has a fourfold etheric aura, with four layers of ether in the atmosphere, and our etheric body is tiny version of that.[59] Our own etheric body is sensitive to the astral influences from this cosmic 'ether-sea', which resonate in the Earth's ether aura.

---

[59] GA 26, p. 224.

The human etheric body maintains the life of the physical body, as well as enabling healing and reproductive powers. Rudolf Steiner taught that it is also the mediator of all sensory impressions to the soul, and it is involved in thinking processes, too. The etheric body also is the medium for our inner perceiving, not just our outer, sensory perceiving. In other words when a human being becomes aware of the presence of a thought, an idea, a memory, then it is the etheric body that is bearing these to the soul.

It is the function of the life-force organism, the ether body, to mediate these as well as impressions of sensory objects, to consciousness. Whether a human being registers the presence of a sensory stimulus or an element of their soul life, or a spiritual being, these are experienced via the intermediary function of the ether body. So the ether body registers an intuitive idea, a flowering bush, a flash of anger or a non-physical (spirit) entity.

But each person's etheric body is different. Rudolf Steiner mentioned in one lecture, without explaining any further, that some etheric bodies have the tendency to light up, to become brighter and brighter, and others have a very strong capacity to bring into expression the 'music of the spheres'. In other words, what is resonating from the planets on the astral level can bring about a response in such sensitive etheric bodies. There is also yet another kind of etheric body which,

> "contains energies which are very foreign to the Earth; rare energies which make a person a poet, artist, a creative type."[60]

However the etheric body has changed over millennia; in the Third Post-Atlantean Epoch, it was larger, that is, it extended further out from the skin, and over-all, was less closely bound to the physical body. Rudolf Steiner reveals that towards the end of the Third Post-Atlantean Epoch or the Egyptian-Mesopotamian Age (2907 - 747 BC), the etheric body had become too expanded, and needed to be drawn in a little.

He told one audience that the famous Indian spiritual teacher, Krishna, was a vessel of the Christ-impulse, a person who was influenced by Jesus from the spiritual worlds. Krishna successfully undertook to limit the expansiveness of the etheric body, and to change its functionality, to enable human

---

[60] GA 165, p.167.

beings to use its energies in the head area, and to assist efforts in attaining to spiritual enlightenment by one's thinking.[61]

Rudolf Steiner also pointed out that in our Age, the etheric body has become too small, somewhat shrivelled up and hardened. If the etheric body in the past was extending too far out from the feet, and reaching into the etheric energies in the soil, now our etheric body is withdrawing too much up from the feet, and becoming too rigid. This is a process that is made worse by materialistic thinking and associated attitudes.

The more ahrimanic thinking predominates the more rigid and shrivelled up does that person's etheric body become. It is a primary truth in anthroposophy, that one's consciousness, the thinking-life especially, directly affects one's etheric body. In particular Rudolf Steiner taught, it is in the area of the feet that this shrivelling up impacts; he stated that if such a condition were to become very strong, then the feet have a tendency to become hardened, like the hooves of an animal. He told the audience that this is why in Goethe's drama, *Faust*, Mephistopheles is shown with hooves.[62]

So the hidden esoteric message behind the myth of Vidar and his shoe, is that the beings serving the Christ-impulse in our Age, seek to prevent this inner shrivelling up of the etheric body, which physically, could perhaps eventually lead to unnaturally hardened feet. It is then an important task of Vidar's, to work against this inner hardening, or drying-out tendency by instilling in the etheric body of spiritually seeking people, influences which assist their consciousness to rise above the various forms of ahrimanic thinking and materialism.

This is what Rudolf Steiner meant when he told his audience in Oslo, that Vidar shall bring about the new clairvoyance. And this is what the Druids meant when they spoke of how Vidar needs a special shoe made from the casting away of hardened parts of peoples' shoes (that is, the feet area of the etheric body). Vidar's influence seeks to make the etheric body make more sensitive in the feet area, and hence more responsive over-all, to spiritual influences.

----

[61] GA 142, lecture, 31st Dec. 1912, p. 87.
[62] GA 158, lecture, 20th Nov. 1914, p. 103.

21 Vidar puts his shoe into the jaws of the Fenris Wolf, destroying him
(10th century, Gosforth church pillar, UK)

Appendix Two: The Celtic prince 'Vidar-like' statue

In 1996, on a hill known as Glauberg in a forested area of Germany, near the town of Glauburg about 30kms north-east of Frankfurt, a very significant Celtic burial site was found. It is about 200 kilometres west of the Pfalzfeld area. The body of a Celtic prince, interred with valuable items, was found in a grave site there. Then shortly afterwards, a very rare discovery was made; a large and impressive statue of a person with unusual features was found deep in the ground. The large ear-forms of the Vidar statue, and the leaf-forms on his forehead, are also depicted here with this person, see illustration 22.

It is generally agreed that this unusual carving depicts the Celtic warrior whose body was found in a royal grave some metres away. It comes from the same era, and the same culture, the La Tene Celts, as the Vidar column. That the prince is shown with large ears similar to those of the Vidar statue, and also has similar interlinking leaves on his forehead does not mean that this is another version of the Archangel Vidar. Rather, it indicates that the prince is being honoured as a powerful man who revered the Celtic gods, and who consequently was depicted with some of their attributes.

Although described in some reports as the most significant Celtic artwork found in Germany, the Vidar column, when considered in its undamaged state, is a much more significant work of art. The quality of this column, artistically and in terms of its cultural significance and esoteric meaning, places it on a much higher level than the somewhat awkward Glauberg carving.

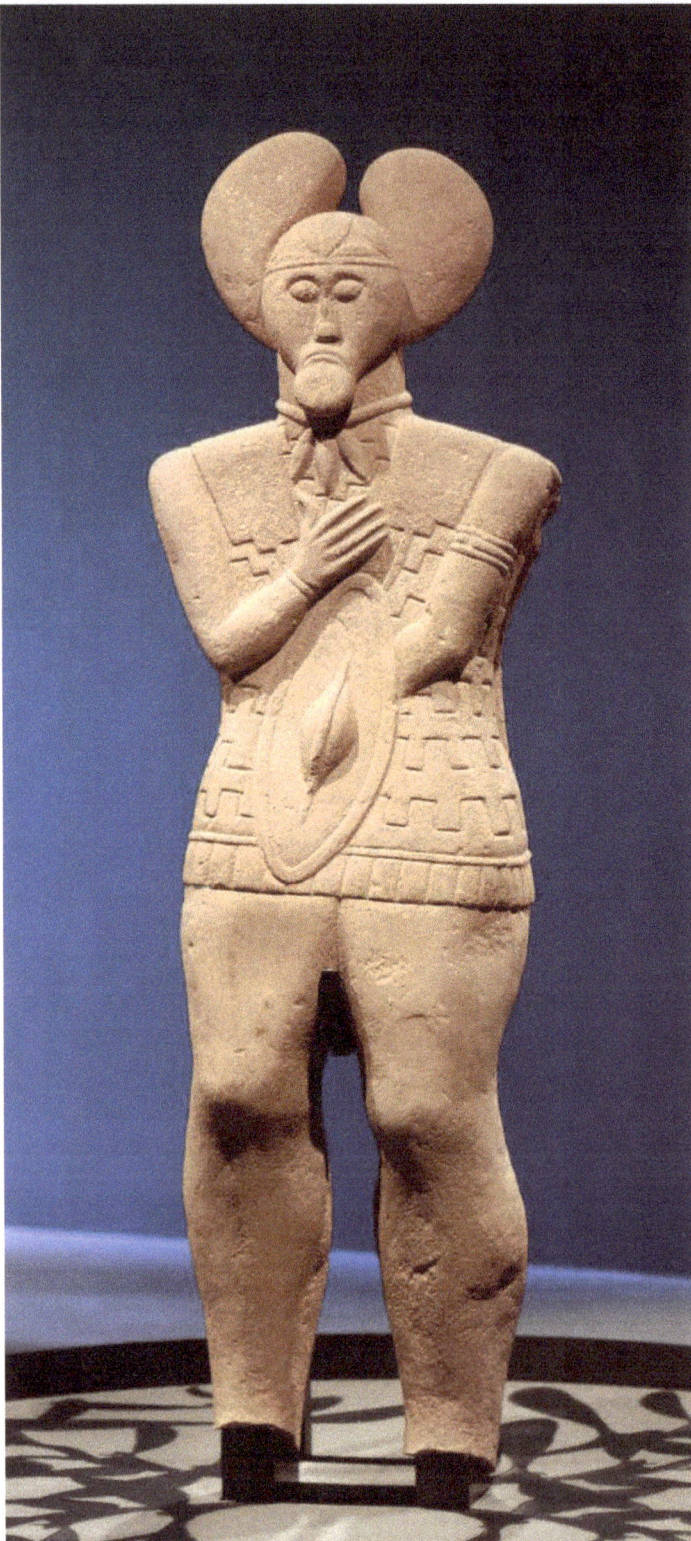

22 The Celtic Prince statue from Glauberg

Appendix Three: References to Vidar in the Edda

1 Loki's Quarrel v.10:

> So get up, Vidar, to make a place
> for the father of the Wolf,
> That never shall Loki speak maliciously
> against us, here in the hall of the Aesir.

2 Loki's Quarrel v.11; the words of Vidar:

> Blessed fortune and well-being, for the Aesir gods
> and the Aesir goddesses !
> and to all of the most sacred gods –
> except for one,
> who is seated further in –
> on the bench of Bragi.

3 The Sayings of Loddfafnir:

> If you have a friend
> who you deeply trust,
> go often, to seek him out,
> for tussocks grow, and long grass,
> in Vidar's forest region.

4 The Voluspa, v. 54:

> Then the great son of the Victory-Father comes –
> Vidar – to fight against the son of the giant,
> with his hand he stabs his sword
> through the gaping jaws, to the heart,
> thus does he avenge Odhin.

5 The Voluspa, v. 55 (fragment):

> Vidar's kin mean death to the Wolf.

6 Hyndla's Song:
> A noble one* came forth to us,   (* Odhin) [63]

---

[63] The old Icelandic text: Varð einn borinn, öllum meiri, sá var aukinn jarðar megni; þann kveða stilli stórúðgastan sif sifjaðan sjötum görvöllum.

greater than all others,
the Earth empowered this son,
He was declared the most endowed of rulers,
Through kin, kinship had he with all the Powers. [64]

One day another shall come forth,
Mightier than he,
But to name him* I dare not,   (*Vidar)
Few now gaze further ahead than
when Odhin encounters the wolf.

7 Grimnir's Sayings v.15:

Tussocks grow and long grass
in Vidar's forest region,
there the son
on the back of the steed
courageously makes it known
he shall avenge the father.

8 Gylfaginning:

Vidar is the name of one of the gods: the silent god.
He has a stout shoe and is nearly as strong as
Thor......
....The Fenris Wolf swallows Odhin at Ragnarok,
bringing his death immediately. Vidar then approaches
the Wolf and places his shoe upon the wolf's lower
jaw. On this foot he has that shoe which is constantly
being formed from the scraps of leather which people
cast away from their shoes, as they are being made;
especially from the toes and heels. Therefore everyone
should cast away those scraps, who is concerned with
helping the gods. With his hands, Vidar then grasps
the Wolf by the upper jaw and tears his snout apart.
And that is the death of the Fenris Wolf. (v.51)

Þá kemr annarr enn máttkari, þó þori ek eigi þann at nefna; fáir séa nú fram
of lengra en Óðinn mun ulfi mæta.
Usually the text reads, "a man was born" but the old Icelandic verb here 'bera'
often has entirely other meanings, such as 'to bring towards', 'raised on high
towards', 'carried forth'.
[64] Usually "...kinship had he with all the tribes/families". But since Odhin was
a deity, spiritual powers are intended here; and the word 'sjölum', old Danish
for spiritual powers (or earthly dynasties) occurs as a reliable variant reading
to sjötum (tribes) in the pivotal Codex Regius.

Appendix Four: References to Vidar by Rudolf Steiner

1: *The Mission of Individual Folk-Souls* lecture cycle, 1910 in Oslo.
   Nearly all references to Vidar by Rudolf Steiner are to be found in this cycle of lectures.

2: Lecture of 21st December, 1913, in Bochum, Germany, on the occasion of the dedication of the Vidar branch there; in GA 150.

3: Lecture of 24th November 1921, in Oslo, at the Vidar branch; in GA 209.

4: Lecture of 21st May 1921, where he also uniquely states that both the southern hemisphere, and the people living in the southern hemisphere have their Holy Nights in the winter time of that hemisphere; in GA 226.

Appendix Five: Contemplating the Holy Grail seal

So powerful and so sacred is this seal (illustration 19) that Rudolf Steiner cautioned about copies of it being placed in mundane areas; it belongs only in a sacred, meditative space. The seal is encompassed by the three Rosicrucian maxims: EDN (from God we are born), ICM (into Christ we die) and PSSR (by the Holy Spirit we are resurrected).

We see, lower down, a cube being permeated by various strands of malignant serpentine astrality, but as we go up, the darkish background becomes light, filled with delicate sparkling radiance. Energies from the two snakes become transformed into radiant spirals of light soaring upwards, to eventually envelope the upwards soaring, golden-white dove.

The dove is entering the upside-down chalice in the throat area of the etheric body, and spreading out left and right from this is a rainbow, but whose colour sequence is incorrect to the physical world. This is probably depicting the colour sequence which the seer beholds in the astral realm.

This image, one of seven, was put on display at an international Conference of the Theosophical Society, held in Munch in 1907, under the auspices of Rudolf Steiner. It is extremely fortunate for us that he did speak about this image on several occasions during the Conference, even if only briefly, and that people did manage to take notes of his explanations. Following are the essential points from these notes, which record some of the most sacred revelations that Rudolf Steiner ever gave. As his comments are not fully recorded, I have added, in brackets and in italics, some explanatory comments,

> "A cube shape, representing the spatial {-physical/mineral} plane, from out of which, on all sides, cosmic serpents issue forth so as to present higher energies which are living through an existence in a lower mode. From the mouths of the serpents are cosmic lines {or pathways} depicted as spirals – the symbol of the purified and cleansed cosmic forces; and arising from these is the Holy Grail, which the dove is facing. All of this is indicating, and actually entirely in accordance with the facts, the secret of the Cosmic Begetting, of which the earthly begetting is but a lower reflection. The deepest mysteries lie in the lines and figures, etc, of this seal."

"When Kama {*lowly sensual astrality*} is under one's feet, then shall the Holy Spirit condition become present. The transparent cube below represents that transparent diamond-cube which consists of carbon. When the human being has spiritually progressed so far that he or she can use the carbon themselves, for the building {and maintaining} of their body – without the participation of the plants – then that person shall produce this cube."

To produce "this cube" is a very brief reference to the theme of transforming, that is spiritualizing, the body, so as to make less dense the heavy protoplasm which has accreted inside the more ethereal, archetypal framework of the body, ever since Lemurian times. In anthroposophy, when a more precise terminology is needed, the 'flesh body' refers to the protoplasm and skeleton, etc, which we can see. Whereas the 'physical body' refers to the ethereal, archetypal framework underlying the flesh body. This theme really is referring to some future age, when human beings shall exist in an etheric body, with only the subtle archetypal form of a physical body still present.

Another feature of the seal are the spiralling lines moving upwards. Rudolf Steiner made only brief comments about these,

"The radiant spirals {*arising from the serpents*} signifies the devotional nature of {*spiritual*} cognizing. Only this devotional, {*non ego-istical*} quality is permitted to comprehend the cosmic spirals in the staff of Mercury, which by then shall be of a fiery kind: they arise forth from untarnished cognizing."

Although here Rudolf Steiner refers to the Staff of Mercury, this Staff is not fully depicted in the seal; only its spirals. The next cryptic passage refers to the actual secret of the holy Grail,

"The plant calyx is today chaste, freely turned up {*towards the firmament*}, but with human beings, it is the reverse situation {*the reproductive organs are not chaste, and face somewhat downwards*}. But the human reproductive area shall again become chaste; it shall also be turned upwards. {*Just how in humans these organs shall be 'turned upwards', is unclear. It may refer to the receiving of in-raying forces from the*} *etheric sun by the larynx, when it becomes the reproductive organ, in a future Age when human beings are again more ethereal and androgynous.}* For this reason is the Grail depicted here as a chalice which is turned downwards. From the larynx there shall be not only that particular power, the power to reproduce, but there shall also be present the power of the fire-spirits *{pyraustas or fire-elementals}. {That is, present as purified energies in the human being's astral and etheric bodies, and under the control of the initiate.}* The pure, chaste human being, the human being who has become innocent, is represented by the dove." *{This is another way of defining the dove; such symbols can be applicable to several levels of meaning.}*

"The purified body of the serpents has a deep meaning...the sun surges on, and in fact, it does this in a spiralling or screw-like motion, with the result that the Earth, {following with the sun}, moves in a complicated motion. The same dynamic also applies to the moon's motions, as it moves around the Earth. You see here how the spirals have their significance amongst the {celestial bodies} in the solar system."

"And these celestial bodies represent a Form with which, at some time in the future, the human being *{once spiritualized}* shall identify themselves...in that future age, the human being shall have purified the reproductive power, shall have cleansed it and at that time the throat and larynx shall become the reproductive organ. The upside-down chalice in us shall become the chalice, which initiates today call the Holy Grail."

"And just as the one element in creation *{the human being}* shall be made chaste, so too shall the other element in creation *{the solar system}* which is in direct connection with the human reproductive power, become chaste: it shall become an essential extract of the Cosmic Spirit *{the solar system's spiritual nature}*. And this Cosmic Spirit, in its essential essence, is depicted here as the dove which is placed near to, or facing, the Holy Grail."

"Here the dove is the symbol of the spiritualized fertilization {process}, a process which is brought about from out of the cosmos, which shall occur once the human being has identified with the cosmos."

That is, once the Grail acolyte or initiate has experienced the "as above, so below" truth. Then the initiate is able to sense, indeed clairvoyantly see, and experience, the union between their own astral body, and the planets.

The next notes from his comments, on a different day of the Conference, take us into especially profound and deep esoteric truths about the mystery of the rejuvenation of the human being through the Christ-reality.

> "The letters EDN {*Ex Deo Nascimur, "from God we are born"*} represent how the human being was, in the beginning, born from out of the 'Primal Powers' of the cosmos."

This title, 'Primal Powers', is one of several titles Rudolf Steiner used for the Archai or Principalities. It is alluding to the colossal truths which he was able to experience and explain in his book *An Outline of Occult Science*, where the Thrones in the Saturn aeon brought forth all things. But in this process the Archai's own evolving was interwoven: as the deepest core or our being, the subconscious will arose, this gave the Archai their own sense of selfhood. So humanity's being and the Archai's own being is interwoven,

> "Every human being, when he or she gazes back, {*finds that they*} have gone through the process in the beginning of time, which today he or she goes through, when they, from out of the capabilities inherent in human consciousness, become re-born."

These are but brief notes, but it seems clear that the main point here is that the sublime process of becoming a 'son or daughter of God', that is, an initiate with the eternal ego born within, is a process which has similar dynamics to that which gave rise to the eternal ego as a slumbering potential, in the Saturn aeon. Actually, it was in the Saturn aeon that the Spirit-human or Atma came into existence, and those who achieve an inner awareness of the Father-principle in creation, are on their way to develop their Spirit-human.

Rudolf Steiner then refers to the three Rosicrucian maxims. We need to realize that ICM stands for, in Latin: "in Christo morimur": in Christ we die. But, as Rudolf Steiner often explained, these letters really mean "**into** Christ we die".[65] He makes this clear in many lectures, e.g., he explains these letters as meaning, "in dem Christus sterben wir", which in English is, "into Christ we die". In Latin this would be "In Christum morimur", not 'In Christo morimur'. To the medieval Rosicrucians this intended meaning was clear, so the dative form 'Christum' was not used. The following brief words recorded in 1907, are meditations, not explanations as such,

> "ICM: {*In Christo Morimur*, "*Into Christ we die*",} In order that he or she finds life again in this death {*process*}, the human being must overcome this sensory death {*by seeking to be renewed*} by the Primal Fountain of all that is living."

The phrase, "this sensory death" appears here in the text without explanation, but one can conclude it refers to the cube with the serpents permeating it. That is, the consciousness that 'fallen' humanity has in the physical world, in terms of sense-bound 'dead' thinking, and also since the Holy Grail is about overcoming of 'eros', sensual desires,

> "And in fact this Primal Fountain {*the Mystery of Golgotha*} is the central point of all cosmic evolution. For {*underlying the entire drama of the purpose of humanity existence is the fact that,*} we **had** to experience death, in order to attain to our {true, eternal} consciousness.
> And we **shall** overcome death when we discover the actual reason for, or the purpose of, this {*fact of*} death {*being part of human existence*} **in the secret of the Redeemer.**"

We can lament that more was not said, or written down, about this last point: "**the secret of the Redeemer**". The person seeking self-initiation on this deep esoteric Christian-anthroposophical path has to meditate upon the phrase,

> "PSSR {*Per Spiritum Sanctum Reviviscimus, 'By the Holy Spirit we are resurrected'.*"}
> There, where a duality manifests, a third element must unite with it. In this way then, shall the human being, when he or she has overcome death, be able to identify

---

[65] He makes this clear in many lectures e.g., GA 143, p. 213.

themselves with the Spirit which permeates creation {symbolized by the dove}."

****

Since a profound aspect of the Holy Grail was inspired by Vidar, we can conclude this Archangel also has an important involvement in the processes which occur in the soul and spirit of the person seeking self-initiation, on the path to the Holy Grail. Rudolf Steiner once told an audience that the purpose of anthroposophy coming into the world could be regarded as encouraging students of anthroposophy to become seekers after the Holy Grail.

This is also implied on many occasions by Rudolf Steiner, including in his book, *An Outline of Occult Science*. Towards the end, he writes of how the "hidden knowledge of the Grail shall become an inner power in the manifestations of life of people; it shall more and more permeate human beings".[66]

---

[66] *Occult Science: an Outline*, p. 407 (German edition), ps. 305-6 English edition, G. & M. Adams translation, 1969.

Appendix Six: A carving mistaken for the Vidar carving

In May 1986, an article was published in the weekly Dornach newsletter of the Anthroposophical Society, *Das Goetheanum Wochenschrift*, by a craftsman, Herr Seufert, which argued that the statue found at Pfalzfeld was not the true Vidar column. Instead Seufert argues that the stone known as the "Niederdollendorf" stone is the right one; see illustration 23.

With regard to the Vidar statue, and the Niederdollendorf gravestone, as the Museum reports, this gravestone is actually a Teutonic (Frankish) chieftain's gravestone, dating from about AD 600; see below for more about this stone. My reply to this article advocating the Niederdollendorf stone, published in a Dornach newsletter from 1986, is given here in a condensed form.

One:
Seufert argued that the Pfalzfeld Column could not have been known to Rudolf Steiner, because in 1910, when Steiner referred to a carving of Vidar, and for many years earlier, it was hidden away in the castle, Schloss Rheinfels. So Rudolf Steiner could only have known about it, if he visited the castle: and so far as we know, he did not.

My reply:
This allegation is factually incorrect. It is well documented by reports and photographs, that from 1845 until 1928, the statue was in the church wall of St. Goar. It was not taken into the castle until after 1928. Rudolf Steiner was in the Rhineland area – visiting Bonn and Cologne – on at least 43 days in the years 1904 to 1910. Also Rudolf Steiner had read the works of Johann Just Winckelmann about German antiquities, and referred to this in his lectures and writings, about 100 times.

On one occasion Rudolf Steiner called him, "one of the greatest German art experts" who inspired Goethe to make some of his most important observations about nature and art.[67] And, as we noted earlier, the announcement about this statue as a La Tene Celtic work was distributed world-wide, through the publication of Koenen's report in 1901.

---

[67] For example, in GA 58, p.159 & GA 271, p.16 & GA 276, p.74 & GA 292, p.227, 232.

Two:
Seufert argued that this statue is a Celtic statue, yet Vidar is a Germanic-Nordic god; so why would the people of one culture depict the god of a different culture?

My reply:
Rudolf Steiner reports that prior to 3,000 BC, the Celts of Europe and the Germanic tribes were different nations or ethnicities. But he then states that after about 3,000 BC these two groups extensively merged.[68] This resulted in the peoples of central and northern Europe becoming, as Rudolf Steiner reports, "Germanic-Celtic people".[69] As historians report, "for the Iron Age, {starting 800 BC} the Celtic element cannot be clearly distinguished from the Teutonic element."[70]

Three:
Seufert argues that since the "Flame column" was found near St. Goar, which is 115 kms from Cologne; it was not "near Cologne" as Rudolf Steiner stated. Whereas the "Niederdollendorf Stone", a Frankish chieftain's gravestone, was found near the village of Niederdollendorf, which is only 35kms from Cologne. Therefore, Seufert concludes, the 'flame column' as the statue was called by Dilich and others, cannot be the right stone.

My reply:
As we noted earlier, Rudolf Steiner was then speaking to people in Oslo which is some 2,000 kms away. The village of Niederdollendorf would have been unknown to the audience in Oslo, but the city of Cologne was the seventh largest city of Germany, and it was a world-renowned city for various religious-cultural reasons. So, the audience away in Oslo would have been able to know the general area of the statue.

Four:
Seufert argues that the Niederdollendorf gravestone is the carving that Rudolf Steiner meant.[71]

---

[68] For example, in GA 180, lecture, 14th Jan. 1918.
[69] He referred to the „keltisch-germanische Bevölkerung Europas"; for example in, GA 161, lecture, 2nd April 1915, GA 180, lecture, 14th Jan. 1918, GA 51, lecture 25 Oct. 1904.
[70] H. Döbler, *Die Germanen, Legend und Wirklichkeit*, p. 269, Orbis press, 2000.
[71] As does S. Prokofieff.

My reply:

Rudolf Steiner stated that the artwork would not be recognizably a depiction of Vidar. The implication of his words being that such a depiction would be recognizable only to an initiate (or in the modern world, someone who had studied anthroposophy). And, as I noted earlier, there is nothing about the 'flame column' which speaks of a god who is fighting a dragon – the prominent feature of Vidar, in the Edda.

However one side of the Niederdollendorf stone is obviously depicting a being struggling against evil powers. In terms of the known figures in the Edda, this someone could be the deity Vidar, or a heroic human being. Either way, this motif here eliminates this stone as the Vidar stone, since the Vidar stone presents features which meant that it would not be recognizable to the ancient Celtic people, nor to modern researchers, as depicting Vidar.

Also, and very importantly, as we noted earlier, Rudolf Steiner makes it clear that this carving was enigmatic to the experts in ancient artwork of central Europe, "no-one knows whom it portrays". In contrast to this, the Niederdollendorf stone is universally identified as a Teutonic (Frankish) artwork, and generally defined as a Frankish warrior's gravestone. That the identity of one of the two persons depicted is unclear, does not alter the fact that in itself, it is not a disputed artwork.

In the next section, the features of this stone are briefly explored.

Appendix Seven: The Niederdollendorf gravestone

In 1901, the same year that Constantin Koenen's expert report on the Vidar column was published, another four-sided carving was found. It was promptly recognized as Teutonic, that is, as a Frankish work of art, dated to about AD 600, and specifically as a gravestone. It was found in a Frankish cemetery near Königswinter in Hesse, which shows signs of being a Teutonic gravesite that was later used by the early Frankish Christians. As it dates from the olden times when there was still some knowledge and psychic awareness of the after-death situation, the stone has some interesting features. But it is not an initiatory depiction of an immensely high deity, who was pre-destined to become an integral part of the Christ-reality.

In contrast to the requirements of the Vidar carving this stone:

* Is a simple, somewhat crude, Teutonic work of art, not an ancient Celtic artwork.

* It has recognizable features of a gravestone; no widespread sensation was caused by its discovery, causing experts to be confronted with an unsolvable enigma.

* It has on one side an after-death scene of a Teutonic warrior struggling in the dismal astral realm.

* On the other side it has a scene which is enigmatic to art historians, but not to the degree of the extraordinary Vidar statue. Some have concluded that the triumphant figure here is Jesus, or a pagan god. Others conclude, as I do, that it depicts the same Teutonic warrior, but now in a better, later part of the after-death journey, (see below).

Such an heroic scene with nuances of conquering evil forces, is precisely what disqualifies it from being the Vidar stone. Because as we have noted above, if the scene is a recognizably heroic one, then it cannot be the esoteric depiction of Vidar, for that depicts his inner hidden spiritual significance, and as such was not obvious to the Nordic-Celtic populace, nor to modern people who know about the Edda today. Those who write about this stone all recognize the heroic, evil-fighting aspect of this scene, see illustration 23.

23 The Niederdollendorf gravestone

Exploring the features of the gravestone

One side shows a human being with a hair comb, in the act of combing his hair. It is well established that most ancient peoples believed that a life-force existed in their hair, and hence the men-folk did not often cut their hair in daily life, in order to maximize their energies. Thus for example, in ancient Greece, men used to comb their hair prior to being in danger, or facing a challenge, for the same reason. This happened when preparing for a battle, or when undergoing an initiation rite (the katabasis).

The Frankish chieftain is holding the wrong end of his sword. The gesture of this feature is saying that he is **entering into a disempowered condition after his death**. Consequently, negative forces are menacing his right hand, that is, his ability to defend himself.[72] As Rudolf Steiner taught, all cultures since the Greco-Latin Age regarded the after-death condition as being, to a large extent, especially in the early stages of existence after death, a dismal time of being disempowered. Hence it is natural that the tribes-people have depicted the warrior as combing his hair, to maximize his power.

He also has a water-flask placed near him. The water flask is a depiction of the real containers placed in such graves to provide food for the journey in the after-life of the soul.[73]

On the reverse side, we see a very different picture. Although crudely drawn, we can see that a person is uplifted and holding a spear. But actually, underneath this heroic entity is not a great Serpent that Vidar might be fighting. Firstly, Vidar did not fight against the Midgard serpent – that was the task of Thor. Secondly, underneath this figure is actually a "Schlangengeflecht", that is, a patchwork of interlaced serpents or malignant energies, not a single serpent: this feature represents the negative astral realms and is referred to in the Edda,

> more serpents dwell under the ash tree Yggdrasil
> than any unwise person can realize ...
> (Sayings of Grimnir, 33)

---

[72] Contrary to Prokofieff, he is not holding his sword anywhere near to his heart.

[73] The theory that this refers to 'purified etheric forces which must permeate the entire system of a person's limbs and metabolism for spiritual triumph' (Prokofieff) is unconvincing.

The image of a 'Schlangengeflecht' is not unique to this gravestone; it directly presents the ancient, widespread understanding that in the Underworld there are many negative beings, whose interweaving in effect constitutes the 'substance' of the lower astral, realms; see illustration 24.

It appears that this triumphant figure is the same Frankish chieftain, in a later phase of his journey after death; and he is shown with three features. One is his spear; he is now empowered, having made his way through the lower astral realms. Secondly, his heart area and the area above the head, is emphasized; this appears to reflect the knowledge that at this later stage, the astral body or aura is now more radiant. It is this same radiance which lights up the surrounding environs; but the environs, whether the 4th or 5th, or 6th astral realm, is itself also more radiant.

A very important, indeed central aspect of existence after death, in the better phases of the astral journey, is the sense of moving ever upwards, of being sustained in this upwards motion and thus able to move ever nearer towards the spiritual sun. The two lines which are near his feet, may also be meant as being underneath him, moving him upwards.

This side of the stone is a positive statement about the stage in the journey of the chieftain after death. The somewhat simple way the figure is drawn speaks not of a god, so much as this same person, but now after he has arisen from the dark lower astral realms, he is now somewhat empowered and is starting to ascend into more radiant realms.

In essence, this is a crudely produced Teutonic carving, readily identified by the relevant researchers as a gravestone for a Teutonic warrior; a Frankish chieftain who lived approximately around 600 AD. It is not an ancient Celtic carving of a revered, mysterious deity.

24 A **Schlangengeflecht** or interweaving of 'serpentine' energies (lower astral forces). Teutonic artwork from the 7th century, found near Halle, in Germany. An heroic Frankish warrior strides over malignant forces, either in life or in the after-life.

Appendix Eight

Vidar in the Edda (Loki's Quarrel): discovering more words from this god

I have presented my research (on pages 19-20) about special words from Vidar, contained in a certain verse from the Edda. But scholars normally regard these words as being spoken by Loki, not by Vidar. The passage is verse 11 in *Loki's Quarrel*.

There are several reason why I regard these words as spoken by Vidar. Firstly, in verse 10, there occurs the extraordinary scene wherein Odhin orders the powerful Archangel Vidar to stand up, away from the table, to thereby allow Loki – who represents evil beings – to join the Gods at their table in the great Hall. For Loki has demanded access to the table of the gods, but he can not gain this access, and thus influence human beings, if Vidar does not retreat.

Now, just before the next verse, verse 11, there is an explanatory sentence which states, "*Then Vidar stood up and offered a cup of mead to Loki; and before he drank, he toasted the Aesir.* Then comes verse 11 which consists of this toast or auspicious greeting;

> Blessed fortune and well-being for the Aesir gods,
> and for the Aesir goddesses,
> and to all of the most sacred gods – except for one,
> who is seated further in, on the bench of Bragi.

This is an auspicious greeting, which I regard as being fully sincere; it is a greeting which is not extended to Bragi, and we shall see why, later. There are various reasons why I have concluded that these words are actually spoken by Vidar, who after this speech becomes silent until the Twilight of the Gods. Firstly, I note that the introductory sentence simply says, *before he drank, he toasted the Aesir.* It does not specify Loki nor Vidar, simply "he" (in Icelandic, *en ápr hann drykki...*); so it is ambiguous. However, it is natural to think that 'he' refers to Loki here; but does it?

There are only three possibilities to support the usual interpretation says that it is Loki speaking here. One view could be that Loki is now sincerely greeting the gods: but this is not believable as the entire text is about his hatred for the

100

gods. The second view may be that Loki is indeed speaking, but is being sarcastic here: however, this not likely either, since he excludes Bragi. Loki and Bragi have already been involved in an argument – so if Loki were speaking and being sarcastic here, then he would all the more want to offer a 'warm' greeting to Bragi also, and not exclude him from the sarcasm. So the third possibility is that, when Loki is allowed to join with the gods, he makes a normal, traditional speech or toast, but nevertheless is still angry with Bragi.

I cannot prove that this third option is wrong, but it is extremely unlikely, for two good reasons. Firstly Loki has had an argument already, not only with Bragi, but also with a god called Aegir or Gymir. Yet at the end of this speech, he excludes only Bragi (if it is Loki speaking); he is happy to include Aegir. So this third possibility makes Loki's behaviour very inconsistent (if he is speaking here). Secondly, the third option is also doubtful because, it is unlikely that Loki would be portrayed as offering even just a traditional, auspicious greeting in the context here, where he is hating and abusing the gods. So I find all three possibilities which could support the Loki theory are unlikely.

My interpretation that it is actually Vidar who is speaking here, does not have these inconsistencies. To me, Vidar here, knowing the enormous importance of this ominous event, makes a kind of 'retreating away' toast, rather than a 'coming and joining you' toast. Hence he made a very respectful and inclusive greeting (both gods and goddesses are included). And, to esoteric insight, his toast also contains an ominous sign. We can discover this sign when we ask, why would Vidar (not Loki) exclude Bragi? Who was Bragi? Bragi is the deity by whom the runes and sacred words which convey the Mystery knowledge to the Druids, is made available to human beings. This power was conferred upon Bragi by Odhin. And it is exactly this which shall be badly harmed by the entry of Lucifer and Ahriman into the world.

Now we need to note that, in verse 11, Bragi is characterized by Vidar as, "one who is seated further in", which means on the special benches with higher status – even though Bragi is not presented elsewhere in the Edda, as being so important. This reference to 'inner benches' and thus a high status to Bragi, shows us that the Mysteries, with their runes and verses, and Bragi's role in all this, **are a very important focus for the speaker**. Loki would have little reason to give Bragi or the Mysteries such a high status. But Vidar would be very focused on both the importance of Bragi, and any threats to the Druidic Mysteries, for Vidar was a central being in the Nordic Mysteries.

Rudolf Steiner taught that Vidar's nature was held secret in the Mysteries because it was so sacred; and Vidar is destined to have a crucial role in re-establishing new Mysteries, after the Twilight of the Gods. So Vidar is very aware that the Mysteries are destined to be harmed by the entry of Loki into the world and also, to be further harmed, some time later, by Loki's offspring, the Fenris Wolf. So Vidar, as he sincerely makes an auspicious greeting here, blessing the gods, cannot in truth and sincerity, include Bragi in his blessing and auspicious remarks.

We need to note also that Loki soon gives a very nasty insult to Iduna (in verse 17); and she is the 'wife' of Bragi. Iduna, as Bragi's 'wife', has an ability which "keeps the gods young"; that is, Iduna represents the power that, through the Mystery wisdom of the Druids, which Bragi is central to, enables human beings to commune with the gods; so the gods don't fade away or 'die', as far as people are concerned. Therefore Iduna too, as an aspect of Bragi's nature, must also soon be a victim of Loki; and so she is.

So, it is my conclusion that in verse 11 we have rare words from Vidar, spoken as he retreats formally from the work of the gods, at a very significant time. As he does so, he extends his blessing to the gods; but since his words are sincere, he has to exclude Bragi from this, for he is very aware that Bragi's future will soon become grim – a sad prelude to the later Twilight of the Gods.

Vidar is speaking here, and giving an omen that the Mysteries, so dependent upon the runes and mantric speech from Bragi, shall be threatened by the entry of Loki to the great Hall. My interpretation of verse 11 is not illogical, is consistent with the role of Vidar, and shows how Vidar responds to the entry of evil in the world. So this verse, viewed as the words of Vidar, is deeply meaningful.

Conclusion

Starting with the statement from Rudolf Steiner that Vidar brings the "central nerve and living essence of all Spiritual Science", we explored all the references to this god in the Edda and all the relevant words from Rudolf Steiner about this being. This led us to contemplate the statue of this deity, carved by the Druids about 500 BC, and first noted officially in the 17th century.

We saw that this deity is an ancient Archangel known in Atlantean times, and who was holding himself back from being involved in humanity's evolution until our times. He became a co-worker with the Christ-impulse in about AD 600, and in medieval times, inspired the most profound definition of the Holy Grail.

We uncovered the trail of historical investigation and interest in this striking carving, which was placed not far from the banks of the river Rhine, in a dense forest area.

With the features of the carving restored, we can see that it indicates two aspects of the Vidar mystery: his ancient phase wherein he was not active, and his modern phase wherein he becomes an important helper of the Christ reality.

Rudolf Steiner's description of Vidar's role in the spiritual rejuvenation of humanity indicates that this deity assists the mysterious and sacred process of the inner 'virgin birth' to occur within the soul-body and spirit-body of the acolyte on the spiritual path.

It became clear that anyone in the modern world who seeks to develop their spiritual potential, in a serious deep sense, is in effect invoking the assistance of this Archangel. The new higher consciousness or clairvoyance arises through the help given by Vidar, and this help brings the spiritual seeker nearer to the Christ reality. It offers this person the opportunity to draw near to the Holy Grail.

Index

Illustration acknowledgements

1: Above left: Freisinger, Sacerdos-Viennensis.blogspot.com
   Above middle: Gosforth cross detail, public Domain
   Wikipedia photo: J. M. Peterson, before 1917
   Above right: Gosforth cross, colour photo: public Domain
   Wikipedia from Doug Sim
   Below: large baptism font in Freudenstadt: public Domain
   Wikipedia from Juergens.mi

2: Above: Tangelgarda Norse stone; Wikimedia: uploaded by
         Dbachmann
   Below left: Wikipedia commons, image by: Gunnar Creutz
         April, 2011
   Below right: Wikipedia Commons (P. Kermode 1927)

3: the author
4: www.orka.bibliothek.universität Kassel, Germany
5: ibid.
6: Rhineland Tourism map
7: From the author's library
8: ibid.
9: the author
10: Above: Schilbach; Museum Georg Schäfer. wikimedia.de
    Below: Schütz; private collection (Koller Auktion A160 lot
    3069, Wikimedia.de
11: Bonner Jahrbuch 1901 (author's library)
12: ibid.
13: Above right: Dilich, portrait by S. Fürck, 1637, published
       in *Bremen im 17. Jahrhundert. Glanz und Elend einer
       Hansestadt,* Wikimedia.de
    Above left: Koenen: photo in Wikimedia.de
    Centre: The Landgraf, Ernst: portrait by Matthäus Merian, in the
       1650s, Wikimedia.de
    Below right: Winckelmann: portrait byAngelika Kauffmann,
       1764. Image from: Emmanuel Giel, 2007, Wikimedia.de
    Below left: The Landgraf, Ernst Leopold: portrait by P. Aubrey,
       date unknown, Wikimedia.de

14: The Rheinisches Landesmuseum, Bonn.
15: The author
16: R. Knorr, in *Germania* journal, 1921, Bamberg.
17: The author
18: Author's library
19: Rudolf Steiner Archives (Public Domain)
20: Public Domain (original in Danish Museum)
21: Detail from the Gosforth cross (Wikipedia)
22: Glauberg figure: Wikimedia; date/ 7 may 2011 / own
       work / E-W / CCA-Share alike
23: Bonner Jahrbuch, 1901
24: Hornhaüser Reiterstein: Wikimedia; Florian 0999 / 9th
       Sept, 2015

Also by this author

Living a Spiritual Year: Seasonal Festivals in Northern and
       Southern Hemispheres   (1992, new edition 2016)
The Way to the Sacred   (2003)
The Foundation Stone Meditation: a new commentary (2005)
Dramatic Anthroposophy: Identification and contextualization of
       primary features of Rudolf Steiner's anthroposophy.
          (Ph.D. thesis, Otago University)   (2005)
Two Gems from Rudolf Steiner: two archive lectures from
       1904 & 1905.   (2014)
The Hellenistic Mysteries & Christianity   (2014)
Rudolf Steiner Handbook   (2014)
Horoscope Handbook - a Rudolf Steiner Approach (2015)
The Meaning of the Goetheanum Windows   (2016)
Rudolf Steiner's Lost Zodiac   (2016)
Rudolf Steiner's Esoteric Christianity in the Grail painting
by Anna May   (2017)

See also Damien Pryor:

The nature & origin of the Tropical Zodiac   (2012)
Stonehenge   (2012)
The Externsteine   (2012)
Lalibela   (2012)
The Great Pyramid & the Sphinx   (2012)

www.ingramcontent.com/pod-product-compliance
Lightning Source LLC
Chambersburg PA
CBHW050819090426
42737CB00021B/3444